THE WORLD TAKES

COLLECTOR'S GUIDE TO TRENTON POTTERIES

Schiffer Publishing Ltd

4880 Lower Valley Road, Atglen, PA 19310 USA

THOMAS L. RAGO

PHOTOGRAPHY BY T. M. RAGO

This book is dedicated to:
—all the hard-working immigrants who risked a great deal to come to this country to start a new life. These men and women toiled long hours for meager wages to pave the way for future generations. My grandparents, Luigi and Filomena Rago were two of these special people.
—my father, Tom Rago Sr., for all he has taught me throughout my life and for all the support he has given me throughout this project.
—my wife, Donna, for being an inspiration in all aspects of my life.

The current price ranges in this book should only be viewed as a guide. The author has assembled his information from a variety of sources including auctions, antique shows, flea markets, and dealer prices. Demand and values for Trenton Potteries artware vary from one part of the country to the next. Neither the publisher nor the author assumes responsibility for any financial gains or losses incurred from consulting this book.

Library of Congress Cataloging-in-Publication Data

Rago, Thomas L.
Collector's guide to Trenton Potteries / Thomas L. Rago; photography by T.M. Rago.
p. cm.
ISBN 0-7643-1277-4 (hardcover)
1. Trenton Potteries Co.--Catalogs. 2. Pottery, American--New Jersey--Collectors and collecting. I. Rago, T.M. II. Title.
NK4210.T7 A4 2001
738'09749'66--dc21
00-012435

Designed by Bonnie M. Hensley
Cover design by Bruce M. Waters
Type set in Windsor BT/Aldine 721 BT

ISBN: 0-7643-1277-4
Printed in China
1 2 3 4

Published by Schiffer Publishing Ltd.
4880 Lower Valley Road
Atglen, PA 19310
Phone: (610) 593-1777; Fax: (610) 593-2002
E-mail: Schifferbk@aol.com
Please visit our web site catalog at
www.schifferbooks.com

This book may be purchased from the publisher.
Include $3.95 for shipping. Please try your bookstore first.
We are always looking for people to write books on new and related subjects. If you have an idea for a book please contact us at the above address.
You may write for a free catalog.

In Europe, Schiffer books are distributed by
Bushwood Books
6 Marksbury Avenue
Kew Gardens
Surrey TW9 4JF England
Phone: 44 (0) 20-8392-8585; Fax: 44 (0) 20-8392-9876
E-mail: Bushwd@aol.com
Free postage in the UK. Europe: air mail at cost.

Contents

Acknowledgements

This book could never have been completed without the concerted efforts of many people. First and most importantly, Martin Winar inspired me and challenged me to undertake this project. From its inception to its completion, he has encouraged me. His knowledge of Trenton and its history afforded me the foundation upon which the text was written.

Next are the Watkinson and Wilson clans. Ed Watkinson, Cate Crown, Steve Nelson, J. Clifford and Verena B. Wilson came into the project when it was already underway. Even though I never met J. Clifford Wilson, I learned a great deal about this Trenton Potteries Co. employee through his wife, Verena, and their grandson, Ed Watkinson. Through a series of fortunate coincidences with Ed, Cate, Steve, and Verena, I was led to some of the most important revelations concerning TEPECO and TAC. Their contributions to this book are immeasurable.

The late Al Bennett, a former president of Trenton Potteries Company, generously recounted his many years at the pottery for me. His kind and gentle demeanor was equaled by his sharp mind. This true gentleman was an inspiration for me and this book.

Two authors who gave me support are Mike Pratt and Harvey Duke. They both assisted me in the research and made me aware of various factors involved in writing and publishing. Their time and insight are greatly appreciated.

Several dealers and collectors opened their homes to me, while others brought me pieces or parts of collections to complete the book. Robin and Carl Cohen have been true partners in this project. Fritz Karch, David Chiacchio, Penny Pypcznski, and Joe Ozga have given generously of their time and collections. "Parker" Prindle has shared information that only someone who has collected Trenton Potteries for decades would have.

Marge Miccio and Robert "Chuck" Wagner, of Artifacts Gallery, were buying and selling Trenton Potteries pieces long before this pottery was fashionable. They are true promoters of the city of Trenton and have assisted me in many ways.

Bob Perzel and Ed Stump are good friends who have done what they could to further my Trenton Potteries collection over the years.

Other dealers and collectors who have shared an interest in promoting the Trenton Potteries story and its artwares include: Neil and Mary Ellen Collins, Howard Auerbach, Gary Zirilli, Jackie Zanca, Roman and Marta Juzeniw, Wayne Oliver and Sheila Klein, and the Brown Bear Antiques shop in Allentown, New Jersey.

A number of people have influenced the development of this project. While there are undoubtedly many more who should be mentioned, this is at least a partial list. Thanks to: Mrs. William Ketchum, Helen Crossley, Joseph Crossley II and his wife Nancy, Ben Whitmire, Main Street Antique Center in Flemington, N. J., Gus Gustavsson, Connie Thatcher, The Trenton Historical Society, Lorraine Kostrzewa, Richard Conti, Danny Downs, Roger Persichelli, Mark Rumbolo, Julie Sferrazza, Ethel and Morris Bruches, Bertha Hoff, Connie Thatcher, Bill Booth, Ed Morgan, Richard Barthold, Renate Rago, Patti Bourgeois and Don Gill, Seymour Lazerowitz, Jim Murphy, Vera Kaufman, David Stout, Ken Rolland, The Potteries of Trenton Society (P.O.T.S.), Gene Pascucci, Arnie Small, George Malcolm, Mrs. Eleanor Hobson and her sister-in-law Mrs. Katherine Jones, John and Debbie Kivenny, David Rago, and Lou Mikolajczyk.

Preface

The Trenton Potteries Company (T. P. Co.) offers beginning and advanced collectors alike a wonderful opportunity to assemble a collection of well designed pottery by shapes, colors, or sizes. Whether you prefer the striking angles and lines of the deco style or the more classical look of Roman and Greek urns, jardinieres, and floor vessels, Trenton has pieces to tempt you. If you like decorating with subtle pastel colors or vibrant blues, greens, and yellows, or contrasting blacks and whites, Trenton offers it all. If your cabinets are large enough only for miniatures, salesmen's samples or vases measuring 5" or less, or if your floors are in need of large urns or floor vases measuring 2 feet or more, Trenton has them.

For the beginning collector and a person with a limited budget, there are a number of items priced in the $25 to $75 range. Also, unusual and desirable vases that are hand painted and pieces with multi-colored glazes are obtainable. Another category for collecting is the advertising pieces Trenton made for various institutions.

Trenton Potteries Company wares are easily identifiable. 95% to 98% of their pieces are marked with one or more of the identifying stamps and labels shown in the marks section. On the rare occasion that an unmarked sample piece or special order item is found, this text will make identification much easier.

If you start a collection of Trenton Potteries wares, you will collect significant parts of New Jersey's rich ceramic history and this nation's proud past.

Pricing

The pricing of any antique or collectible is a challenging task. The values reflected in this text result from the author's many years of experience as a dealer and collector.

Price ranges for the pottery take into consideration desirability and relative scarcity as well as geographical differences. Other factors that impact Trenton Potteries Co. pricing are their color and condition.

Color

The vast majority of Trenton Potteries Company giftware has a single color. The most commonly found colors are Gloss White, India Ivory, Persian Red, and Turquoise Blue. These are all glossy (high glaze) finishes. Less frequently found are matte (flat) or semi-gloss finishes. Therefore, any matte or semi-gloss finish commands 20% - 100% over the price ranges of the common glossy pieces. Highly desirable colors such as Cobalt Blue, Mirror Black, Purple, and Rose can surpass value ranges by 50% - 150%. See pages 29, 49, 53, and 82 for examples.

Decal applied, hand painted, dual or multi-color pieces are priced individually based on their scarcity and aesthetic appeal.

Condition

All the values here reflect Trenton Potteries Company wares that are in "mint" condition, where "mint" refers to pieces with only very minimal wear that are free from any flaws or damage such as glaze misses, uneven glaze, chips, hairline cracks, and surface scratches.

Introduction

The Great Depression and World War II opened and closed a significant chapter in the annals of the Trenton Potteries Company. The production of vitreous clay artware and giftware defined a scant ten-year period, from 1932 to 1942, in which a previous world leader in the production of sanitary ware and plumbing fixtures was forced to reshape the company to survive economically. How the company met this opportunity is illustrated in the following pages and sheds light on an era that defined itself in various ways.

From strong linear Deco shapes to traditional and Neo-Classical Roman vessels, Trenton Potteries' ingenuity is evident. With a cast of ordinary workers and industrial designers and artists including Henry Dreyfuss, Harriet Curwin, Elisabeth Brown, and G. McStay Jackson, among others, the Trenton Potteries embarked on creating uniquely exciting wares that are highly sought after today.

Through this book it is the author's intention to provide better understanding of why "TRENTON MAKES, THE WORLD TAKES."

A photograph of the bridge in the new millennium. While the bridge has not changed much, Trenton's industrial production has diminished greatly during the last half century.

A decal on a Wenczel Tile Co. (Trenton, N. J.) ashtray depicts the "Trenton Makes" bridge. Above the bridge is the outline of the capitol and beneath the bridge is a potter at his wheel. The slogan refers to Trenton's industrial production during the early and mid-twentieth century of which the sanitary ware and pottery businesses were among the largest and most important.

History

Ceramics History in Trenton, New Jersey

Trenton's rich ceramic past can be traced back to Native Americans who inhabited this part of central New Jersey. A broad belt of rich clay deposits in Trenton and surrounding areas made pottery making feasible. The best known early potteries in the Trenton area date back to the late 18th and early 19th centuries. A recent archeological dig by Hunter Research unearthed a nearly intact kiln built by William Richards in the late 1700s. More potters from England followed. By the mid-1800s, skilled craftsmen from Ireland and Germany had also settled in Trenton.

The clay that had once been used for making basic earthenware vessels was now being formed into dishes, hotel ware, sanitary-ware (commodes), tiles, bricks, and other general wares. By the 1870s and early 1880s, Trenton was the national center for the ceramics industry.

By the end of the 19th century, however, Trenton had been supplanted as the largest producer of clay products nationally by the Ohio regions in and around Zanesville. A number of work strikes and shut-downs had disastrously beset the Trenton companies. Nevertheless, Trenton was still making specific ceramics products; it was the first and leading producer of "Beleek" and fine china in this country. The names John Hart Brewer, William Bromley, Jonathan Coxe, Isaac Broome, and Walter Scott Lenox are synonymous with the initial venture and production of "Beleek" ceramics in the United States. Roughly at the same time, Thomas Maddock was the first successful manufacturer of sanitary-earthenware in the United States. By 1897, Thomas Maddock and Sons was producing sanitary-ware from vitreous china. By the late 19th and early 20th centuries, Trenton was home to the majority of sanitary-ware companies in America. The growth of the pottery trade, both general and sanitary wares alike, depended on surviving the crippling union strikes as well as the sweeping tariff reductions for foreign-made wares which were enacted during President Grover Cleveland's administration.

This photo depicts part of a large metal engraving plate with TEPECO's Trade Mark Registration patented Nov. 4, 1902. The number 1 under the star probably indicates the first of several trade mark variations. Note that each point on the TEPECO star symbolizes each of the five merging potteries.

Trenton Potteries Company, Founded 1892

During these historic times, the Trenton Potteries Company (TEPECO) was founded. Several allied industries combined in 1892 when the Crescent, Delaware, Empire, Enterprise, and Equitable Potteries joined to become Trenton Potteries Company. This formidable company could compete against English-made sanitary wares.

In 1904, at the St. Louis World Exposition, TEPECO was awarded a grand prize for its sanitary wares. From that point forward, TEPECO fixtures were used by builders worldwide. Tourists traveling the globe are said to have seen TEPECO fixtures as far away as the Imperial Hotel in Tokyo and grand hotels in Paris and Berlin. At one time their plumbing and bathroom fixtures were in the Presidential Palace in Havana and the White House in Washington.

Under the leadership of John A. Campbell, the pottery continued to thrive during the first two decades of the 20th century. As general manager from 1897 until 1908 and president until 1932, he led the company through predominantly prosperous, yet challenging times.

A Trenton Potteries Company advertisement issued by The Board of Trade City of Trenton, N. J. U. S. A. (1900) indicates the vast product line of sanitary earthenware items for sale. A world leader had been created in only eight years. *Courtesy Mike Pratt*

THE TRENTON POTTERIES COMPANY,
TRENTON, NEW JERSEY.

THE LARGEST SANITARY EARTHENWARE MANUFACTURERS IN THE WORLD.

PLUMBERS' SANITARY WARE DEPARTMENT, VIZ.: Syphon Jets and Hoppers, Washouts and Pedestals, Basins and Urinals, Crockery Flush Tanks, in Regular Ware and also Vitreous China.

SOLID PORCELAIN BATH AND LAUNDRY DEPARTMENT. Bath and Laundry Tubs, Kitchen, Pantry and Slop Sinks, Lavatories, Foot and Seat Baths, etc., etc.

RAILWAY AND STEAMSHIP DEPARTMENT, VIZ.: Closets, Hoppers, Urinals and Basins for Cars, Steamships and Yachts.

Also large producers of GENERAL WARE AND SPECIALTIES, VIZ.: Dinner, Tea and Toilet Sets, Umbrella Stands, Pedestals and Jardinieres.

Also W. G. and Semi-Granite Ware (full line). Vitrified China. Druggists' Sundries and Hospital Requisites.

All the above either plain white or decorated.

THE TRENTON POTTERIES COMPANY.

D. K. BAYNE, PRESIDENT.
WM. S. HANCOCK, VICE-PRESIDENT.
J. A. CAMPBELL, GENERAL MANAGER.
C. E. LAWTON, SECRETARY AND TREASURER.
E. C. STOVER, ASSISTANT GENERAL MANAGER.

These 1920-1922 ads from House + Garden magazine capture a period of
innovation and prosperity for TEPECO. An air of confidence and superiority
punctuate these ads for various bathroom, kitchen, laundry, and toilet needs.

An enamelware sign from the early 1900s that might have been on the doors or fences of one of the plants during the strikes or lockouts.

Two further ads show that, despite the Crane takeover, little change occurred within the manufacturing and advertising at the Trenton Potteries Co. The ad on the left is from April, 1921, and the ad on the right is from September, 1924.

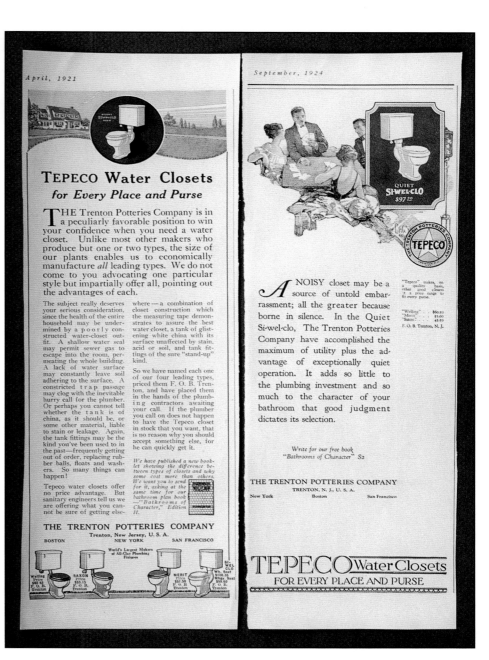

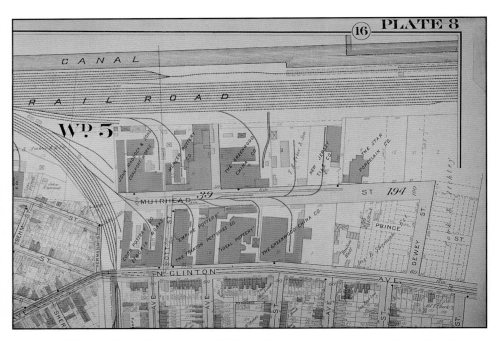

A map of Trenton Potteries Company, 1900, and surrounding potteries. Note that the Empire Pottery still is listed separately, despite being one of the five potteries making up TEPECO.

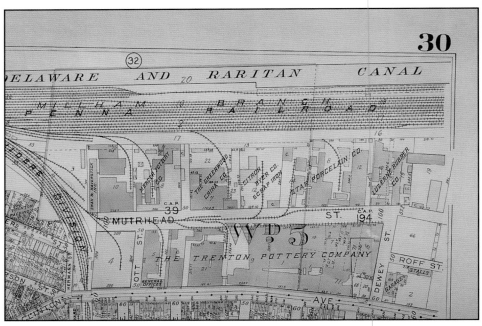

A map of Trenton Potteries Company, 1930, by Franklin Survey Co. of Philadelphia. Under the Crane Company, the pottery covered one full city block.

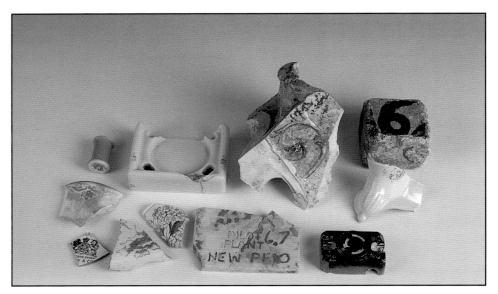

A recent pottery dig by the author at Plant #1, 309 North Clinton Avenue, uncovered various shards.

A Superior Fire Linings Co., Trenton, N. J. brick from Plant #1. It may have been part of an old Trenton Potteries Co. kiln.

A 1927 "Insurance Map of Trenton, N. J." published and updated by the Sanborn Map Company of New York showing Plant #2 at Lalor and Hancock Streets. Note that this map shows the Equitable Pottery, Plant #5. Despite making up part of the Trenton Potteries Co., the Equitable Pottery was listed in directories until after 1941.

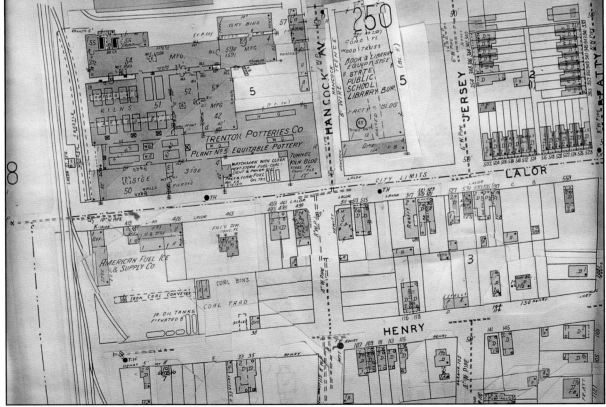

A TEPECO bathroom fixture in Persian Red, probably from the 1920s-1930s.

A Trenton Potteries Co. Christmas dinner party in 1924 with minstrel show. *Courtesy Ed Watkinson*

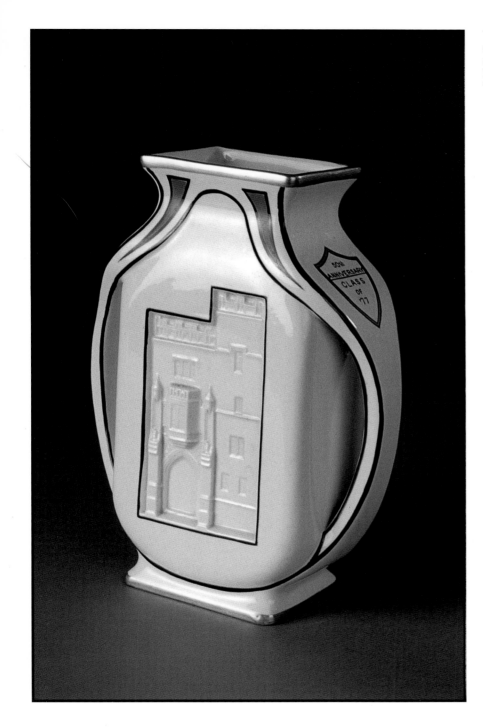

This extremely rare vase, found in the home of a former employee who worked at the pottery during the mid-1920s, is decorated in Princeton Tiger orange and black. Painted on both shoulders are the words: "50th Anniversary Class of '77." *Courtesy Ed Watkinson*

Both front and back panels of this vase have apparent depictions of two different buildings at Princeton University. The intaglio and relief work on the panels is exceptional and must have required the finest craftsmanship to produce. *Courtesy Ed Watkinson*

The TRENTON POTTERIES Co.

THE WORLD'S LARGEST MAKERS OF ALL-CLAY PLUMBING FIXTURES

TRENTON, N.J., U.S.A.

BRANCH OFFICES:
BOSTON
CHICAGO
NEW YORK
SAN FRANCISCO
PHILADELPHIA

July 2, 1928

Mr. Calvin R. Hunter
111 N. 30th St.
Penbrook, Harrisburg, R.D. #5, Pa.

Dear Sir:

A copy of our new Blue Book of Plumbing that you requested is being mailed you today by insured parcel post.

This book contains our complete line, including every modern type of plumbing fixture. In it you will find the latest sanitary, hygienic and mechanical improvements in modern plumbing from which complete plumbing specifications can be written for every type of building without the need of referring to several catalogs.

In this book we have endeavored to illustrate and describe each and every fixture in such a way as will enable you to make a selection and prepare your plumbing specifications in the easiest and quickest possible manner. The descriptions accompanying the illustrations may be copied directly into your specifications with the assurance that every detail is adequately covered.

The various sizes and overall dimensions of all fixtures are given at the foot of the page, together with such roughing-in measurements that are needed in planning the arrangement of fixtures.

Any fixture may readily be located by the quick reference index at both the front and back of the book.

As we have forwarded you literature from time to time and your request for this catalog is evidence that you are reading our "ads" in the Architectural Publications, we know you are familiar with the recognized quality of "Tepeco" Plumbing Fixtures, but we wish to again remind you of our guarantee on page X of this new edition. This will assure you that we still and will continue to maintain the same high standard of excellence that has established a preference for our product wherever the best is required.

Our method of marketing and other general facts in regard to our product are given on page VI but should there be any additional information you may desire, please write us and we shall be very glad to forward it.

Yours very truly,

THE TRENTON POTTERIES CO.

M. W. Lansing
Advertising Manager

MWL I

This July 2, 1928, letter indicates that branches had opened up throughout the northeastern corridor as well as in Chicago and San Francisco. *Courtesy Ed Watkinson*

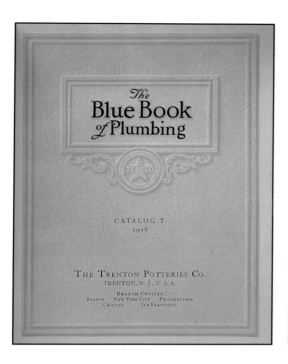

The
Blue Book
of Plumbing

TE·PE·CO

CATALOG T
1928

THE TRENTON POTTERIES CO.
TRENTON, N. J., U. S. A.

BRANCH OFFICES
BOSTON   NEW YORK CITY   PHILADELPHIA
CHICAGO   SAN FRANCISCO

INDEX

AERIAL VIEWS
THE TRENTON POTTERIES CO.
TRENTON, N.J.

The Plant and the Product

To the average person, the home of "Te-pe-co" All-Clay Plumbing Fixtures *is impressive* because it covers an extensive acreage. Yet to those familiar with Trenton's early pioneering in the interests of improved sanitation and advanced utility and design, the size of the present-day plant is not nearly so impressive as are the things that size signifies.

The progress of The Trenton Potteries Company has been great, but it would be wrong to assume that this progress has been rapid. For pottery making is an art—and art is long. Perhaps no other industry has faced greater obstacles or overcome more difficulties in perfecting its production. And certainly few have depended so largely upon that same spirit of pride in craftsmanship which created and kept alive the "Guilds" of a former day.

This Guild spirit; this striving for perfection which brought The Trenton Potteries Company to the fore, is the thing about our factories in which we take real pride. You will see it in the faces of our men; you will find it reflected in the work they do. It is the cornerstone upon which our great plant has been erected—the "priceless ingredient" in the products we manufacture.

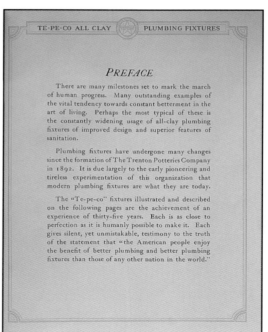

PREFACE

There are many milestones set to mark the march of human progress. Many outstanding examples of the vital tendency towards constant betterment in the art of living. Perhaps the most typical of these is the constantly widening usage of all-clay plumbing fixtures of improved design and superior features of sanitation.

Plumbing fixtures have undergone many changes since the formation of The Trenton Potteries Company in 1892. It is due largely to the early pioneering and tireless experimentation of this organization that modern plumbing fixtures are what they are today.

The "Te-pe-co" fixtures illustrated and described on the following pages are the achievement of an experience of thirty-five years. Each is as close to perfection as it is humanly possible to make it. Each gives silent, yet unmistakable, testimony to the truth of the statement that "the American people enjoy the benefit of better plumbing and better plumbing fixtures than those of any other nation in the world."

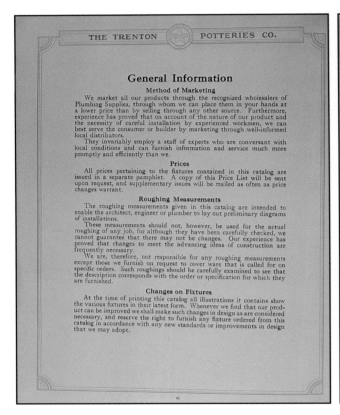

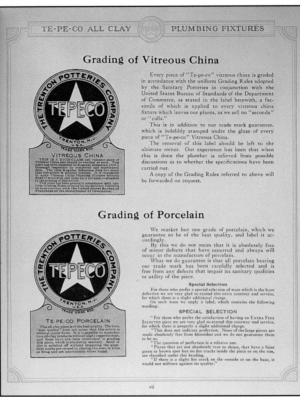

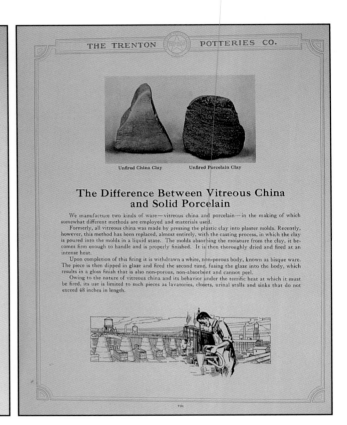

Left page (vi)

General Information

Method of Marketing

We market all our products through the recognized wholesalers of Plumbing Supplies, through whom we can place them in your hands at a lower price than by selling through any other source. Furthermore, experience has proved that on account of the nature of our product and the necessity of careful installation by experienced workmen, we can best serve the consumer or builder by marketing through well-informed local distributors.

They invariably employ a staff of experts who are conversant with local conditions and can furnish information and service much more promptly and efficiently than we.

Prices

All prices pertaining to the fixtures contained in this catalog are issued in a separate pamphlet. A copy of this Price List will be sent upon request, and supplementary issues will be mailed as often as price changes warrant.

Roughing Measurements

The roughing measurements given in this catalog are intended to enable the architect, engineer or plumber to lay out preliminary diagrams of installations.

These measurements should not, however, be used for the actual roughing of any job, for although they have been carefully checked, we cannot guarantee that there may not be changes. Our experience has proved that changes to meet the advancing ideas of construction are frequently necessary.

We are, therefore, not responsible for any roughing measurements except those we furnish on request to cover ware that is called for on specific orders. Such roughings should be carefully examined to see that the description corresponds with the order or specification for which they are furnished.

Changes on Fixtures

At the time of printing this catalog all illustrations it contains show the various fixtures in their latest form. Whenever we find that our product can be improved we shall make such changes in design as are considered necessary, and reserve the right to furnish any fixture ordered from this catalog in accordance with any new standards or improvements in design that we may adopt.

Middle page (vii)

Grading of Vitreous China

Every piece of "Te-pe-co" vitreous china is graded in accordance with the uniform Grading Rules adopted by the Sanitary Potteries in conjunction with the United States Bureau of Standards of the Department of Commerce, as stated in the label herewith, a facsimile of which is applied to every vitreous china fixture which leaves our plants, as we sell no "seconds" or "culls."

This is in addition to our trade mark guarantee, which is indelibly stamped under the glaze of every piece of "Te-pe-co" Vitreous China.

The removal of this label should be left to the ultimate owner. Our experience has been that when this is done the plumber is relieved from possible discussions as to whether the specifications have been carried out.

A copy of the Grading Rules referred to above will be forwarded on request.

Grading of Porcelain

We market but one grade of porcelain, which we guarantee to be of the best quality, and label it accordingly.

By this we do not mean that it is absolutely free of minor defects that have occurred and always will occur in the manufacture of porcelain.

What we do guarantee is that all porcelain bearing our trade mark has been carefully selected and is free from any defects that impair its sanitary qualities or utility of the piece.

Special Selection

For those who prefer a special selection of ware which is the least defective we are very glad to extend this courtesy and service, for which there is a slight additional charge.

On such ware we apply a label, which contains the following wording:

SPECIAL SELECTION

"For those who prefer the satisfaction of having an EXTRA FINE SELECTED piece we are very glad to extend this courtesy and service, for which there is properly a slight additional charge.

"This does not indicate perfection. None of the large pieces are made absolutely free from blemishes and we do not guarantee them to be so.

"The question of perfection is a relative one.

"Pieces that are not absolutely true to shape, that have a faint green or brown spot but no fire cracks inside the piece or on the rim, are classified under this heading.

"If there is a slight fire crack on the outside or on the base, it would not militate against its quality."

Right page (viii)

Unfired China Clay   Unfired Porcelain Clay

The Difference Between Vitreous China and Solid Porcelain

We manufacture two kinds of ware—vitreous china and porcelain—in the making of which somewhat different methods are employed and materials used.

Formerly, all vitreous china was made by pressing the plastic clay into plaster molds. Recently, however, this method has been replaced, almost entirely, with the casting process, in which the clay is poured into the molds in a liquid state. The molds absorbing the moisture from the clay, it becomes firm enough to handle and is properly finished. It is then thoroughly dried and fired at an intense heat.

Upon completion of this firing it is withdrawn a white, non-porous body, known as bisque ware. The piece is then dipped in glaze and fired the second time, fusing the glaze into the body, which results in a gloss finish that is also non-porous, non-absorbent and cannot peel.

Owing to the nature of vitreous china and its behavior under the terrific heat at which it must be fired, its use is limited to such pieces as lavatories, closets, urinal stalls and sinks that do not exceed 48 inches in length.

Courtesy Ed Watkinson

The names of the "Cast of Entertainers" are written on the back of the photo on the next page, presumably by accounting employee J. Clifford Wilson. His notes indicate that 250 people were present at the Contemporary Club on West State Street in Trenton. *Courtesy Ed Watkinson*

A June, 1929, Annual, "TE-PE-CO Outing on the Delaware River." The office employees are shown and Al Bennett, former company president, identified their names, as written on the back.

Despite the tumultuous times that lay ahead for TEPECO, a group of office
employees celebrated Christmas 1929 in playful fashion. *Courtesy Ed Watkinson*

Pages from an undated "TE-PE-CO Plumbing Fixtures in Color" (circa 1920-1925) brochure outlining some of the color options available to customers. *Courtesy Ed Watkinson*

OLOR *in Bathrooms....*

With the introduction of colors in plumbing fixtures, it is no longer necessary to be content with a bathroom that simply meets every sanitary requirement. No longer need one tolerate the austerity of the conventional all-white bathroom that heretofore has been accepted as a practical necessity. Now the decorative treatment of the bathroom and the beauty of its appointments may be made just as distinctive as anything which enters into the design and equipment of the home.

Color has transformed this room from one of utilitarian plainness into one of actual beauty—one that reflects the individuality and taste of the owner just as much as the furnishings of his living room.

In delicate tints that blend delightfully with modern colored tile, Te-pe-co Fixtures in pink, lavender, yellow, blue, ivory and green, afford the most striking and beautiful color effects imaginable. In perfect harmony with any decorative scheme one may prefer, they provide the utmost in beauty with no sacrifice in sanitation, for every Te-pe-co Fixture regardless of its color or design carries the same guarantee of durability and quality.

Thus, without impairing the sanitary excellence of the modern bathroom, Te-pe-co Colored Plumbing Fixtures introduce unlimited possibilities in lending that personal expression and charm of distinction to the decorative scheme of the bathroom which is so apparent in every other part of the home.

MODERN COLOR EFFECTS

Our experience in carrying out various color schemes has proved that it is practically impossible to secure a pleasing effect by attempting to match the color of the plumbing fixtures with other bathroom furnishings and surroundings. Seldom is such a color treatment as beautiful, cheerful or interesting as can be obtained by the artistic blending of several harmonious colors, and we earnestly recommend that the decorative scheme of the bathroom be handled accordingly.

MARBLEIZED CHINA—the newest creation in plumbing fixtures—introduces a charm and distinction in bathroom treatment of which the eye will never tire. In the natural colorings and delicate veinings of Botticino and other marbles, matched with rare skill and enriched with the gleaming lustre of genuine Te-pe-co Vitreous China and Porcelain, it harmonizes admirably with whatever treatment of walls and floor you may prefer. To the beauty of marble is now combined the unequalled sanitary and enduring qualities of china.

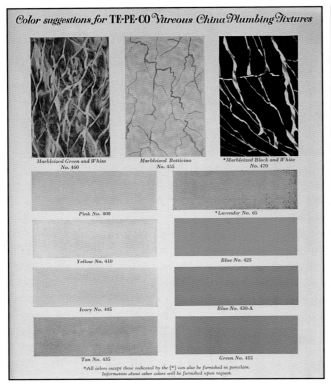

Color suggestions for TE·PE·CO Vitreous China Plumbing Fixtures

Marbleized Green and White No. 460

Marbleized Botticino No. 455

Marbleized Black and White No. 470

Pink No. 400

**Lavender No. 65*

Yellow No. 410

Blue No. 425

Ivory No. 405

Blue No. 430-A

Tan No. 435

Green No. 415

All colors except those indicated by the [*] can also be furnished in porcelain. Information about other colors will be furnished upon request.

OUR GUARANTEE

The Trenton Potteries Company makes but one grade of ware—the best that we can produce—and sells it at reasonable prices. We sell no seconds or culls. Our ware is guaranteed to be equal in quality and durability to any sanitary ware made in the world. The Te·pe·co trade mark is found on all goods manufactured by this Company and is your guarantee that you have received that for which you have paid.

The Colors shown in this folder match the colors of Te-pe-co Vitreous China Plumbing Fixtures as closely as the printing art permits. In fact, the slight variation that exists between these colors and our ware is even less than the variation in the color of the ware itself. As variation in the color of earthenware is unavoidable, we do not guarantee to exactly match these colors. Neither do we guarantee an exact match of any fixture with others that may be called for on the same order or subsequent orders.

THE TRENTON POTTERIES COMPANY
TRENTON, NEW JERSEY, U. S. A.

Te-pe-co Porcelain Kitchen Sinks and Laundry Tubs are now being furnished in delicate tints and marbleized effects. To the sanitary perfections of Te-pe-co Solid Porcelain and Vitreous China is now added the charm of color—tones that blend with whatever decorations your taste may dictate.

Those housewives who have had the opportunity of testing the relative enduring qualities of Te-pe-co ware and other materials realize full well how much more easily dirt and grease can be removed from its surface and how much more durable that surface is. These sanitary and economic qualities will be found in like degree in Te-pe-co colored ware.

THE TRENTON POTTERIES COMPANY
TRENTON, NEW JERSEY, U. S. A.

Exhibit Rooms:
101 Park Ave., New York City
Entrance on 41st Street

Offices in Boston,
Philadelphia and San Francisco

TE·PE·CO
ALL CLAY PLUMBING FIXTURES

Tunnel Kilns and Slip Casting

Two major innovations occurred during the early 1920s that affected pottery and sanitary-ware production. First was the introduction of tunnel kilns in 1922 that rapidly replaced outdated beehive kilns. Because the tunnel kilns ran continuously, productivity rates were greatly increased. The second modernization involved the use of slip casting in place of the much slower and generally less efficient process of pressing clay into molds.

With modernization came labor unrest. In 1922 and 1923, prolonged "lockouts" in most of the potteries in Trenton were at least partially due to reactions against the modern techniques implemented by the sanitary-ware companies. During this period, the Crane Company of Chicago obtained a controlling stock interest in TEPECO, and on April 17th, 1924, they obtained control of the plants. However, the TEPECO trademark did not change and John A. Campbell continued to be the president of Trenton Potteries Company. Under the new ownership, the company was enlarged. The property next to the Empire Pottery was purchased and a new plant was built. This large, new plant became known as Plant #1, at 309 North Clinton Avenue. Plant #2 was located at Lalor and Hancock Streets. (Today this location is occupied by a strip mall and shopping center.)

The next few years at the "enlarged" Trenton Potteries Company plants were prosperous. Trenton Potteries ventured into their first experimentation with vitreous china artware in 1927. Not since the 1904 St. Louis Exposition, where four large hand painted and decorated urns were displayed, had vitreous china artware been written about or seen. John Campbell, an 1877 Princeton University graduate and now longtime president of the pottery, may have commissioned his company to produce the magnificent 10" vase to commemorate the 50-year anniversary of the class of 1877 (see Back Cover and page 15). How far and fast the company evolved under John Campbell is further illustrated in a letter to a customer in Harrisburg, Pennsylvania (see the illustrationon page 16) and the accompanying *Blue Book of Plumbing* (1928). The introductory pages from Catalog T (see the illustration on pages 17 & 18) demonstrate the company's proud but challenging past that had led them to a prosperous and exciting present in 1928. What lay ahead for John Campbell and his Trenton Potteries as the decade came to an end would again change the face of this company and the industry as a whole.

The stock market crash of October, 1929, and subsequent Great Depression had a crippling effect on Trenton's vitreous plumbing and sanitary ware products. With a proven work force and skilled management, modernized equipment, and quality products, the company, as they had in the past, had to somehow meet the challenge.

TEPECO Art Ware

In 1932, at the end of company president John A. Campbell's illustrious forty-year career, a new direction began for the pottery. To keep laborers out of unemployment lines and the fires burning in the tunnel kilns, TEPECO introduced a new product line: artware and giftware. With an array of already existing sanitary ware glazes, both in single colors and marbleized finishes, TEPECO now had to design the art wares. According to former Trenton Potteries president Al Bennett, many of the shapes for vases and smoking related items were designed in-house during the early TEPECO vitreous china years.

The first ads for the art wares that appeared in 1933 already displayed a substantial line of "high grade china vases." Trenton Potteries had showrooms in New York City, Philadelphia, and Trenton. As is evident from the advertisements, the company's initial venture into art china seems to have been fast-paced and successful.

Trent Art China (TAC)

By the mid-1930s ads for a new division of the Trenton Potteries Company, Trent Art China (TAC), had been created. While it is unclear whether TEPECO and TAC coexisted in their china ware production, TEPECO ads for artware seemingly disappeared in the mid-1930s while ads for Trent Art China continued into the early 1940s.

The transition from TEPECO vases to Trent Art China vases must have had economic as well as image reasons. As can be seen from the ads, the unit prices fell when the focus shifted to volume sales (by the dozen). Also, the most expensive marbleized chinaware items were not marked under the TAC name and single color options were minimized as well. Under the new division, there were six, and later seven, in-stock colors available. The new division put more distance between the old sanitary ware and the new artware products. No longer were the vases, planters, and urns a means to survive tough economic times; the TAC wares were making a strong statement by themselves.

During the second half of the 1930s, Trent Art China designed strong Deco style shapes that rival the best Deco pottery in the world. Three industrial designers who influenced production during this period were G. McStay Jackson, Henry Dreyfuss and Harriet Curwin. Al Bennett recalled how Henry Dreyfuss came to Trenton on several occasions with an assistant and "left a lot of the details for his assistant to handle." Henry Dreyfuss also did industrial design work for the parent company, Crane, during this period.

A very early TEPECO six-sided and multi-faceted 12" deco vase in Venetian Blue glaze. The initials (T. F. or C. F.) are unknown, but the 1932 date is significant. This indicates that artware production had commenced at least by 1932. $200-$300

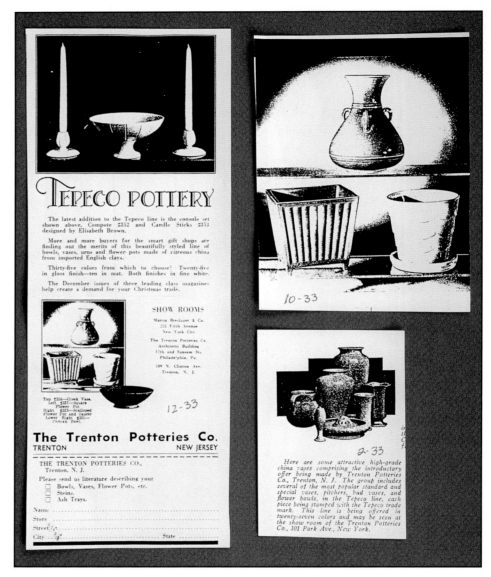

A February, 1933, advertisement with "introductory offer" for a group of high-grade china vases. A December, 1933 advertisement offers a console set designed by Elisabeth Brown. Note that in the February ad, there were 27 glazes to choose from and by December there were 35 different glazes. *Courtesy Harvey Duke*

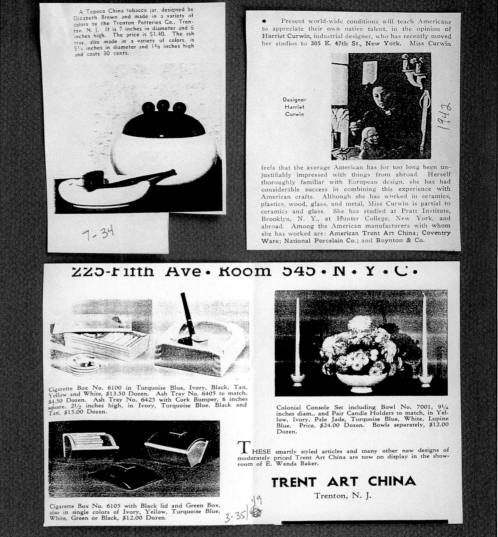

Two further advertisements for TEPECO wares from late 1933. Many of the designs were then being created by Elisabeth Brown. In an ironic twist, the ad on the right touts that the clays used in the china wares are imported from England. Note that the urn at the top right sells for $1.00-$1.50 in single color glaze, but for a marble glaze costs over $5.00. Maybe this is why marbleized pieces are extremely rare. *Courtesy Harvey Duke*

A July, 1934, TEPECO china tobacco jar advertisement designed by Elisabeth Brown, followed by a March, 1935, Trent Art China ad for smoking accessories and other artware. A short biographical sketch of industrial designer Harriet Curwin, who worked at TAC, is also included. *Courtesy Harvey Duke*

pieces from the Trent Art China line, division of the Trenton Potteries Co., which line is now being shown by E. Wanda Baker, 225 Fifth Ave., New York. These pieces were shown recently at the 22nd Annual Flower Show, New York, and are reported to have been outstanding sellers. They are priced from 50 cents to $1.50 and are all made of genuine vitreous china, a material that compares favorably to fine table china. The line is stocked in 6 colors, the complete range of colors including 17 gloss finishes and 6 matt finishes. Each item is obtainable in any of these shades at a slight extra charge if it is not a stock color. Every piece is guaranteed against crazing and the glaze and body are seep and water proof, as well as being guaranteed against stain or discoloring.

Two TAC ads from the mid-1930s with the contact person being E. Wanda Baker in New York City. Note that under the new American Trent Art China lines, there are now six stock colors and only a total of 23 different colors. *Courtesy Harvey Duke*

Trenton Potteries Co. worker's pay stubs from 1945. After the war, jobs were plentiful and backlogged orders had to be filled.

As America's involvement in World War II became a reality, the corporate focus was turned once again to sanitary wares and other needs of the military. During these war years vitreous chinawares were discontinued. By 1945, when the war was over, a huge backlog of orders for sanitary wares and plumbing fixtures consumed the production schedule.

The Crane Company

In 1950, Trenton Potteries Company became a division of the Crane Company that is based in Chicago. Within two decades, after more strikes, crippling fires, and an increasingly competitive marketplace, the Crane Company closed their Trenton operations in 1970. What remains today is a rich tradition and history that has touched the lives of many Trenton Potteries employees and customers.

Colors

Color is one of the primary factors that identifies Trenton Potteries products. The TEPECO line offered 27 colors in 1932, and at the end of 1933 their advertisements mentioned 40 color choices, including ten in matte finishes. Very few art or vitreous china companies in the United States offered that array of solid colors.

By the mid-1930s, under the TAC line, Trenton Potteries had curtailed their range of colors to 17 gloss finishes and six matte finishes. A June 1, 1941, American Trent Art China price sheet lists only seven colors in-stock.

Only a few of the colors advertised can currently be identified with certainty. The most conclusive list of color variations is found in an early TEPECO brochure and price sheet listing 27 colors. While some of these colors are easily identified, the variations in blues, greens, and browns are particularly challenging to decipher. A few recently uncovered sample color tiles have solved part of the mystery concerning TEPECO glazes.

As the line changed from TEPECO to TAC, some of the colors were dropped, some were continued, and some were added. In 1941 the remaining seven in-stock colors included:

India Ivory #405
Persian Red #485
Cobalt Blue #550
Gloss White #680
Turquoise Blue #682
Spring Yellow #689
Twilight Green #719

Two of the least commonly found Trenton Potteries Co. colors include a matte black and glossy purple vase. As discussed on page 23, the pottery scaled back their color selection, probably due to economic pressures. Therefore, some of the TEPECO colors are difficult to find today. The combination of a rare and attractive glaze can easily double the value of a piece.

Undated color and price sheet of TEPECO wares.

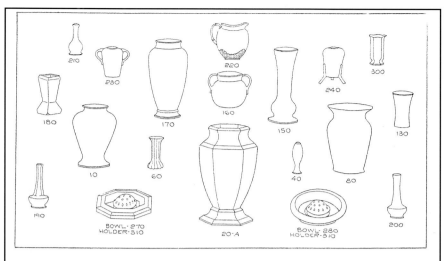

TEPECO COLORS

Tepeco Vases are made in a variety of twenty-seven colors, ranging from the lightest to the darkest shades of green, blue, red, purple and brown.

India Ivory	No. 405	Apple Green	No. 655	Purple	No. 635
Citrus Yellow	No. 410	Nile Green	No. 420-A	Royal Purple	No. 640
Sky Blue	No. 625	Palmetto Green	No. 441	Sun Tan	No. 495
Marine Blue	No. 660	Evergreen	No. 630	Light Brown	No. 610
Venetian Blue	No. 430-A	Orchid Pink	No. 665	Light Mottled Brown	No. 605
Oxford Blue	No. 620	Rose	No. 670	Dark Mottled Brown	No. 600
Lisbon Blue	No. 445	Persian Red	No. 485	Chocolate Brown	No. 615
Pale Jade	No. 415-A	Lavender	No. 490	Black	No. 450
Fern Green	No. 418	Burgundy	No. 645	Pearl Grey	No. 650

UNIT PRICE LIST OF TEPECO VASES

In choice of above colors, F. O. B. Trenton, N. J.

No. 10 Standard Vase, 12" high	$4.00	No. 180 Square Vase, 8" high	$1.20
No. 10 Standard Vase, 18" high	9.00	No. 190 Mayfair Bud Vase, 8" high	1.00
No. 10 Standard Vase, 22¾" high	20.00	No. 200 Laverne Bud Vase, 8" high	1.00
No. 20 Trentonian Vase, 12" high	4.00	No. 210 Aleda Bud Vase, 7" high	1.00
No. 20-A Trentonian Vase, 18" high	9.00	No. 220 Water Pitcher, 8¼" high	2.50
No. 40 Akron Bud Vase, 6" high	1.40	No. 230 Two-Handle Jug, 6¾" high	2.00
No. 60 Fluted Vase, 6" high	1.00	No. 240 Three-Leg Vase, 8¼" high	2.30
No. 80 Peony Vase, 13" high	4.50	No. 270 Octo. Flower Bowl, only, 10" overall	1.50
No. 130 Tumbler Vase, 7" high	1.00	No. 280 Round Flower Bowl, only, 10" overall	1.50
No. 150 Thistle Vase, 15" high	4.00	No. 300 Hex. Flower Vase, 9" high	1.80
No. 160 Rose Bowl, 7" high	2.70	No. 300 Hex. Flower Vase, 6" high	1.20
No. 170 Empire Vase, 16" high	6.00	No. 310 Improved Flower Holder	.50

TEPECO VASES

In a variety of colors and designs the artistic simplicity and sterling quality of Tepeco Vases introduce a new standard of beauty in the decorative appointments of a home. They are especially designed to adequately display and accentuate the beauty of flowers, but without this touch of nature are none the less objects of beauty that will enhance the appearance of any environment.

Tepeco Vases are made of identically the same china as Tepeco Bathroom Fixtures. Beneath the brilliant sheen and colorful surface of a non-absorbent glaze the vitreous china body insures a permanency of finish that will never change. Neither the glaze nor body will seep nor absorb water. Glazed both inside and outside, they are absolutely impervious, and are guaranteed not to stain, craze nor discolor.

THE TRENTON POTTERIES CO.
TRENTON, N. J.

Twelve color sample TEPECO tiles. *Courtesy Ed Watkinson*

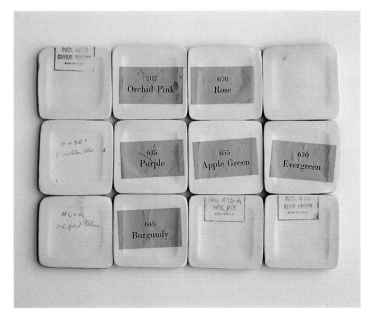

The backs of the twelve sample tiles
and the colors they represent.

Detail of the reverse sides of the color tiles.

6" Purple TEPECO #40
Akron bud vase with gold
rim. *Courtesy Ed Watkinson*

10 1/2" TEPECO Matte Black ring vase with two handles. *Courtesy Joe Ozga*

Trenton Potteries Company Marks

The following marks have been found on items of Trenton Potteries artware and vitreous china. While exact dates are difficult to determine since fires at the factory just prior to the plant closing destroyed most of the company records, a feasible chronological order has been established. Only two "Crane" marks are known on Trenton pieces.

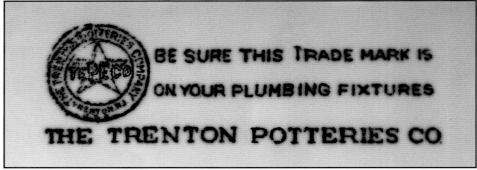

A TEPECO mark found on a salesman's sample advertising plumbing fixtures. This mark may have been used for an extended period of time, 1920s-1940s. *Courtesy Joe Ozga*

A TEPECO mark with the #6 under the star and the TRADE MARK REG. lettering above the circle. This mark was found on a battery casing and probably predates the production of artware and giftwares, 1910s-1920s.

Found on the bottom of an ashtray which also has been seen with a standard TEPECO mark, this "Compliments of Trenton Potteries Co." mark is not common, 1920s-1930s. *Courtesy Penny Pypcznski*

A silver and black paper label found on a pitcher and mug set, 1932-1935.

A final TEPECO ink stamp mark on a piece of vitreous ware, 1932-1935.

A TAC (Trent Art China) ink stamp on the bottom of a vase, 1935-1942.

An American Trent Art China sticker on a bud vase, 1935-1942. The TAC ink stamp and stickers were used jointly or separately.

During the TAC production period, artware pieces were decorated in gold. Some appear to have been decorated in-house, while others were sent to decorating companies. A Stouffer Fine China ink stamp accompanies a TAC stamp, late 1930s to early 1940s.

A Wheeling Decorating Glass and China mark on the bottom of a Trent Art China shaped vase, late 1930s to early 1940s.

This Crane Co. 80-year anniversary stamp was found on the bottom of a yellow Trenton ashtray.

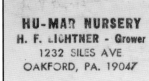

This Crane No. 485 Persian Red ink stamp, on the bottom of a TEPECO line vase, may have come from either the initial period of pottery making, 1931 to 1932, or possibly at the end of their production when the artware was being phased, 1940 to 1950s.

A TAC mark with the rare mark of the nursery and owner with whom Trenton Potteries Company apparently conducted business, late 1930s to early 1940s.

Ashtrays, Boxes, and Smoking Accessories

After the successful introduction of cigarettes to soldiers during World War I, smoking had become a regular feature of civilian life during the 1930s and 1940s. Trenton Potteries produced many ashtrays and cigarette boxes to accommodate this trend.

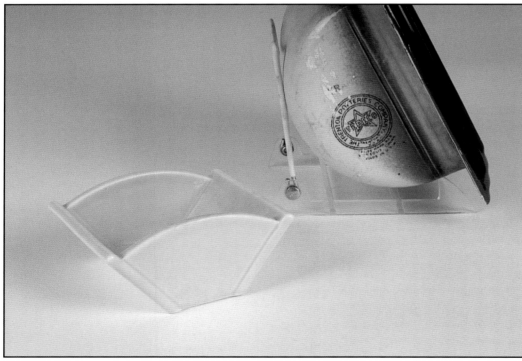

An India Ivory cigarette box with TEPECO mark. The rounded lid with handle is missing from this box. The box is 4 1/2" wide by 3" high with lid. With lid $60-90, without lid $30-45

5" wide TEPECO advertising ashtrays. These are not commonly found and usually have some gold or paint wear. $75-125 each

Turquoise Blue Deco TEPECO ashtray, 3 1/2" wide x 1" high. $50-75

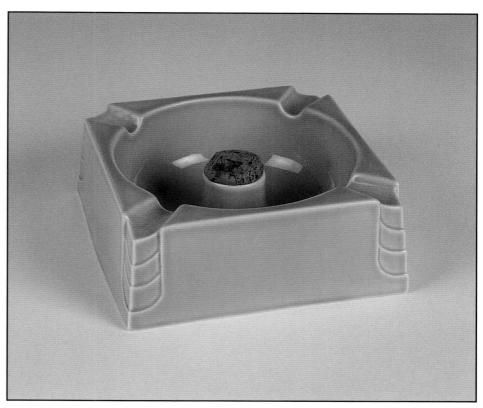

Large TEPECO ashtray in Turquoise Blue, 6" wide x 2 1/2" high, with interior cork to empty tobacco from a pipe. $75-100

Two TEPECO ashtrays in Apple Green and Fern Green. Ashtray on left
has match holder and measures 5 1/2" wide x 2 1/2" high. $50-75.
Six-sided, star-shaped ashtray on right is less common. $60-90

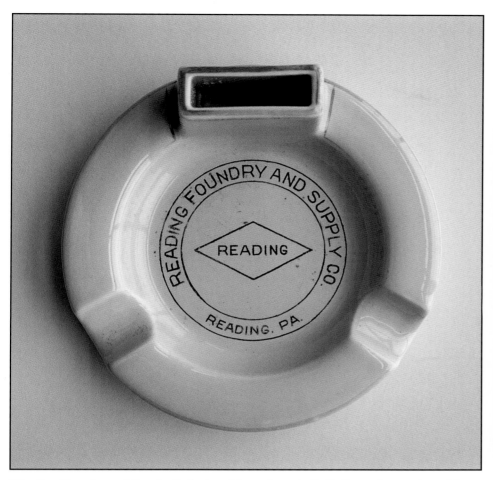

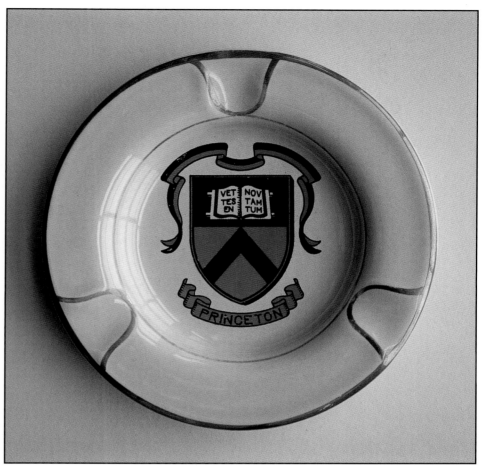

"Reading Foundry and Supply Co." advertising ashtray in India Ivory. A rare piece, this shape is identical to the Apple Green ashtray on the previous page. *Courtesy Ed Watkinson* $100-150

Princeton University logo on the same shape as shown at left without match holder. *Courtesy Ed Watkinson* $75-125

Four ashtrays or bowls, all measuring 5 1/2" diameter and 1 1/4" high. The
Oxford Blue in the front and Citrus Yellow ashtrays have a TEPECO mark. The
Oxford Blue and salmon colored ashtrays have TAC marks. $50-75 each

A Pale Jade TAC Deco ashtray, 3 1/2"
diameter and 1 1/4" high, with two
apparent single cigarette holders. *Courtesy
Martin Winar* $60-90

Two strong Deco-shaped, TAC marked, ashtrays. These two smoking items capture the style
of the 1930s period. The flaring cigarette holder and ashtray on left is uncommon and
measures 4 1/4" in diameter. $75-100
The salmon colored round ashtray with rings measures 3 1/2" in diameter. $50-75

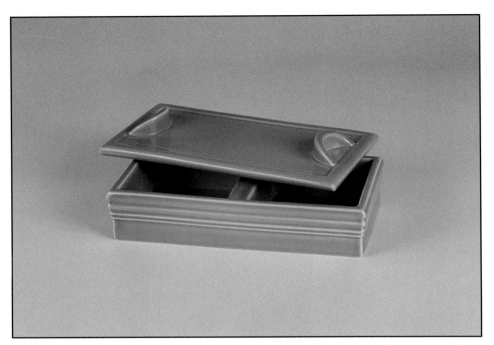

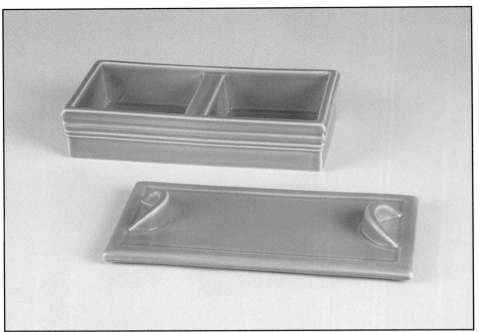

Two views of a divided cigarette box with ear handles. The first shows the lid on the box and the second shows the lid separate from the box and the divider inside. This TEPECO box is 8" long x 4" wide x 3" high. $100-150

A rare floral decorated box with horn-of-plenty handle on lid. This TAC box has floral decals with a hand-applied gold finish. 6" long x 4 1/4" wide x 3 1/2" high. $100-150

Console Bowls and Candlesticks

A fashionable statement in home decorating popularized during the 1930s-1940s was the centerpiece with candlesticks. Trenton Potteries was able to capitalize on this trend and designed numerous console bowls, footed bowls, compotes, and matching candlesticks. Mixing and matching among the bowls and candlesticks appears to have been a practice.

This unusual TAC ribbed console bowl with matching candlesticks in Persian Red measures 8 3/4" x 3" for the bowl and the candlesticks are 2 3/4" high. *Courtesy Martin Winar* Bowl $75-125 and candlesticks $60-90

This TEPECO set, complete with flower frog in Mirror Black, is quite rare. The round flower bowl measures 10" diameter with the flower holder measuring 3 1/4" high with 2 1/2" candlesticks. *Courtesy Martin Winar* Bowl $50-75, flower holder $20-30, and candlesticks in common colors $40-60. Add at least 50% to these prices for mirror black.

10" x 2 3/4" octagonal flower bowl with possibly matching 3 1/4" candlesticks. Ironically, the bowl is marked TEPECO and the candlesticks TAC. Bowl $60-90 and candlesticks $30-45

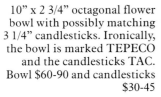

9" ribbed #351 bowl with #353 candle holders in Gloss White with gold trim and TEPECO marks, designed by Elisabeth Brown. These candle holders are common with both TEPECO and TAC marks. Bowl $60-90 and candlesticks $35-50

Dark Mottled Brown TEPECO bowl and candle holders are a match, but include the #280 bowl and #353 candle holders. Bowl $50-75 and candlesticks $30-45 in common colors. Add up to 50% more for this color.

A Gloss White TAC console
set with detailed deco lines.
These pieces are uncom-
mon and quite handsome.
Bowl $75-125 and candle
holders $60-90

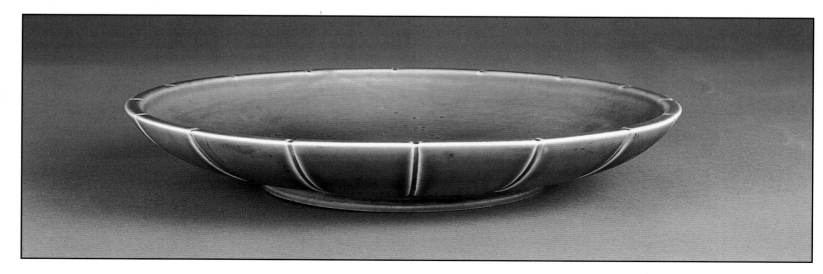

Elisabeth Brown designed
the low bowl with TEPECO
mark in matte medium
blue; it measures 13"
diameter x 2" high.
Courtesy Martin Winar $75-
125

Three more #351 bowls by Elisabeth Brown in TEPECO colors of matte medium blue, Rose, and Apple Green. $60-90 per bowl in common colors. Add up to 50% more for these uncommon colors.

A Venetian Blue, Elisabeth Brown designed compote with TEPECO mark measuring 9" in diameter by 5" high. Note the subtle differences between the low bowl and other bowls shown previously and this compote. $75-125. In premium color add up to 50% more.

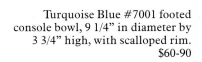

Turquoise Blue #7001 footed console bowl, 9 1/4" in diameter by 3 3/4" high, with scalloped rim. $60-90

Large #530 TAC low bowl with subtle flower and leaf motif measuring 11 1/2" in diameter, designed by Harriet Curwin. $75-125

A very basic 10" low bowl with TEPECO mark in an India Ivory glaze. $40-60

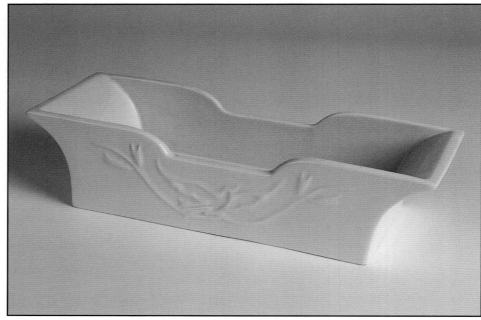

A six-sided, 12" x 4" Deco shaped console bowl with a TEPECO mark in a light blue matte glaze. $100-150

A 12" x 4 1/2" Gondola centerpiece with TAC mark. This flaring bowl has a stylized dove and branch motif. $100-150

An Apple Green, 12 1/2" x 3 1/2", flaring and footed console bowl with TAC mark. $60-90

Two pairs of TAC candlesticks in common colors Turquoise Blue and Persian Red. The candlesticks on left are 5" tall with great Deco lines and have been seen as part of set with the Gondola planter shown on the previous page. $75-125 the pair
The candlesticks on right $60-90 the pair

The most common Trenton candlesticks in a rare pale pink TEPECO color and common Persian Red. Pink $60-90 and red $30-45 the pair

Three pairs of candlesticks in yellow, white, and black. The yellow and black pairs are marked TEPECO and the #518 white pair is marked TAC. They measure 2 1/4", 3", and 2 1/2" respectively. In common colors $40-60 a pair or up to $60-90 for uncommon to rare colors

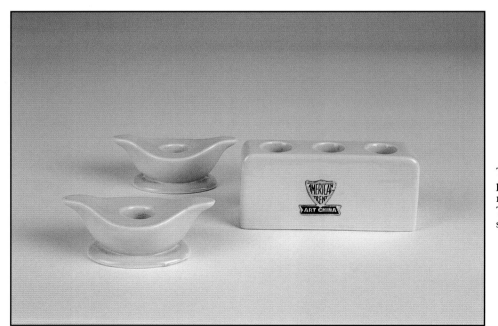

Two India Ivory TAC candle holders. The pair of single candlesticks on the left measure 4" x 1 1/2". $40-60 pair
The individual triple Block holder measures 5" x 2 1/4". $50-75

Cornucopias

Trenton Potteries' cornucopias were produced in relatively large numbers at an affordable price. They are readily available today and still fairly inexpensive.

Three different No. 4005 cornucopias, measuring 6" high, with TAC marks. On left is a matte cobalt blue, in center a matte medium blue, and on right a glossy Cobalt Blue. $25-35 each in common colors, add 50% to 100% to these values for any of these blue colors.

Two additional 6" cornucopias with varying decorating styles. The front left piece with gold overlay was decorated at the Wheeling plant. The piece in the rear has India Ivory glaze with a fine floral and gold trim. $50-75 each

The Verde cornucopias have a Neo-Classical design. They are 4" high and are all marked TAC with a grape motif $30-45 each

These #212 cornucopias, measuring 5 1/2" in height, are less commonly found than the 6" or Verde cornucopias. The fine gold with floral decoration commands a premium over the Gloss White piece. With decoration $50-75 and without decoration $35-50

This largest and most impressive Citrus Yellow cornucopia measures 9" tall and is found infrequently. $100-150

Drinking Vessels:
Mugs, Pitchers, and Tumblers

Trenton Potteries' position in the drinking vessel market was limited. Despite their 1933 advertisement for steins and pitchers (see page 25), these items are not easily found today. Decorated pitchers and mugs are truly uncommon. Tumblers, on the other hand, can be found and occasionally carry a U.S.N. (United States Navy) ink stamp. All items in this chapter have a TEPECO mark, and some tumblers have been found unmarked. This may indicate that the Trenton Potteries Company dropped out of this competitive market sometime during the mid-1930s.

An 11 1/2" India Ivory pitcher and a 5" Oxford Blue stein. Pitcher $100-150 and stein $35-50

A very rare 7-piece pitcher and mug set in mirror black. $500-750

Three tumblers, each measuring 3 3/4". Pale Jade $30-45, U.S.N. tumbler $40-60, plain white $20-30

Four tumblers with a 1/4" lip. These 4" tumblers are less common than the 3 3/4" tumblers. *Courtesy Martin Winar* U.S.N. Tumbler $50-75, others $25-35 each

The underside of the 4" U.S.N. tumbler indicates an early TEPECO mark. Could these tumblers have been used during World War I? Due to the highly sensitive nature of military contracts, it is difficult to ascertain during what period tumblers were a military contract item. *Courtesy Martin Winar*

Frogs, Flower Frogs, and Flower Holders

One of the few multi-colored glaze pieces of Trenton Potteries is their TEPECO figural frog planter. This frog is hard to find, is highly sought after, and has plenty of attitude! The four colors that make up our friendly frog are Fern Green, Citrus Yellow, White, and Black.

Straight-on frog

In-your-face frog

Is this his better side?...   ...or is this side better?

Rigor mortis frog. The four colors that make up our friendly frog are Fern Green, Citrus Yellow, White, and Black. $300-450
Until recently we did not know that the "4-color frog" had relatives. These same 8" x 4 1/2" single-color frogs are rare, but not as aesthetically pleasing as "attitude frog."

These TAC marked frog planters are in India Ivory and glossy white. *Courtesy Ed Watkinson* $250-350 each

There's that frog again! Flower frogs below:
Persian Red $20-30 and for Mirror Black $35-50

This Turquoise Blue Flower
Shell with built-in flower frog
measures 10" x 8 3/4" with a
TAC mark. $60-90

These two #9050 Paradise flower frog vases are 5" high with berries and leaf motifs. They are both TAC ink stamped. Turquoise Blue $40-60 and Cobalt Blue $75-125

Lamps

How many lamps did Trenton produce and sell? It appears the answer is not too many, on both counts. The limited availability today and small number found in the past, indicate that lamps may have been special order items. This is also the conclusion of Eleanor Jones Hobson, who worked at the North Clinton Street Plant #1 from about 1935 until 1941. As a production line worker, she sanded the vases before a color glaze was applied. She does not believe that lamps were a standard production item.

The pottery appears to have implemented a logical production strategy. With the exception of the lamp shown on page 63, all the lamps were identical in shape and size to the vases. The only difference was factory-drilled holes and an occasional modification to the base for the electrical cord. Hardware was added, a bulb was put in the socket, and you had a lamp. Trenton Potteries lamps are highly sought after and command a premium over identical vases today.

This #354 TAC urn lamp has gold trim on the handles, top rim, and near the base. It stands 8" tall and has a modified base. $75-125

Opposite page

Left: This 7 1/2" lamp in Persian Red is identical to the vase on the right except for the drill hole. Both are ink stamped TAC. Lamp without hardware $60-90, with original hardware $75-125, and the vase $40-60

Right: This "Circlet Lamp" in India Ivory with original hardware and finial is an unusual find. From top to bottom this lamp measures approximately 20". The ceramic vase measures 9" in diameter. *Courtesy Martin Winar* $180-275

This rare 10" Persian Red lamp has heavy felt on the base so a TEPECO or TAC mark has not been established. With the apparent original shade, this piece measures over two feet tall. *Courtesy Ed Watkinson* $300-400

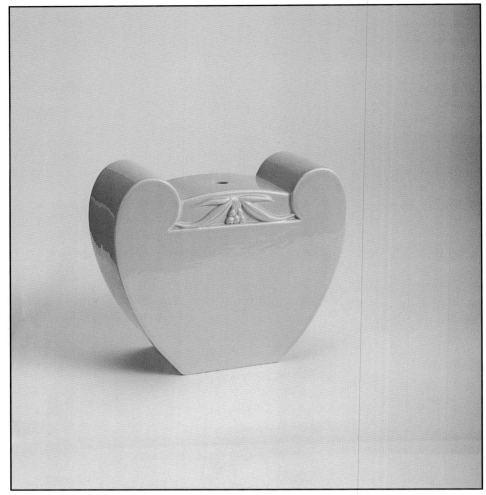

This 12" urn lamp in white with gold trim is an exciting decorative piece as a vase or lamp. It is almost never seen as a lamp. *Courtesy Ed Watkinson* $200-300

7" India Ivory Cameo lamp with modified opening in the top for factory drill hole. This lamp has yet to be seen with fitted hardware. *Courtesy Penny Pypcznski* $100-150 and with hardware $125-175

Planters, Flower Pots, and Jardinieres

A wide variety of shapes, sizes, and colors define Trenton Potteries Company's planters, flower pots, and jardinieres.

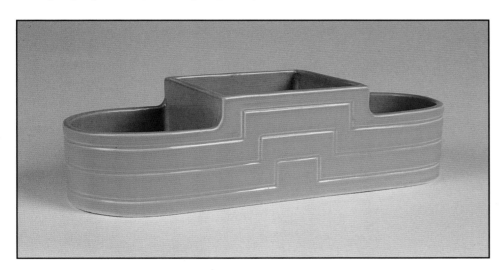

This Sky Blue Fantasy planter designed by G. McStay Jackson measures 13" x 4 1/2" and has a strong Art Deco appeal. The Sky Blue color is a shade more blue than the Turquoise Blue and is rare. Sky Blue $140-200. Value for common colors $100-150.

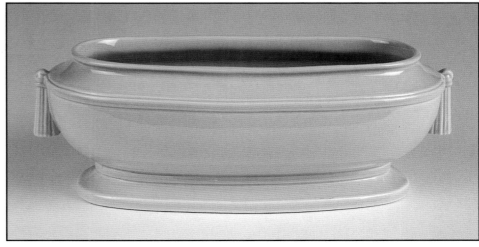

This 12" x 4 1/4" TAC planter in India Ivory with tassel handles is elegant, yet subtle. Presumably, they were sold individually or as a set. $75-125

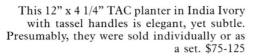

These Twirl planters in Turquoise Blue and Apple Green measure 6 1/4" x 3" each and are stamped TAC. $50-75 each

This #516 planter or bowl in India Ivory is 12" long. $60-90

Opposite page:
This 10" x 5" TEPECO planter in Persian Red is rounded into six individual surfaces. $75-125

This grouping of five 7" Ivy Bowl planters displays an impressive array of Trenton colors. In the front is a Spring Yellow (TAC) planter. In the second row on left is a Mottled Brown (TEPECO) piece and on the right is a Sun Tan (TAC) piece. In the third row is an Orchid Pink (TEPECO) planter and in the back is a Cobalt Blue (TAC) pot. Yellow $25-35. All other pieces $35-50

A 10" Persian Red Ivory Bowl and 7" Cobalt Blue planter. 10" piece $50-75

A 7" flaring TAC flower pot with a separate under-plate in India Ivory. This Deco set was well used (staining on the base). Flower pot $60-90 and under plate $10-15

This 7" TAC flower pot with integral saucer in Apple Green has a ribbon band near the top rim. $75-125

The Square Pot series, designed by Elisabeth Brown, was made in five sizes. These footed planters have four tiny feet and are fragile. The white pot measures 4" and the ivory pot 7". 4" $25-35, 7" $40-60, and square saucer $10-15

Opposite page:
These four flower pots, designed by Elisabeth Brown, range in size from tiny to extra large. Trenton produced five different sizes measuring from 3" to 9". The pots shown are Gloss White 3" TEPECO, Turquoise Blue 4" TEPECO, Rose 6" TEPECO, and Gloss White 9" TAC. 3" $20-30, 4" $25-35, 6" in Rose $60-90, 9" $60-90, and saucer $10-15

This small 5" Jardiniere with gold trim handles and a Persian Red floral design on an ivory body is fairly uncommon. $50-75

These two TAC 7" Jardinieres both have gold trim. The piece on left has a Chocolate Brown floral design on an ivory body and the piece on right comes in a desirable Oxford Blue glaze. $75-125 each

Opposite page:
Trenton's Jardiniere came in two sizes: five inches and seven inches. These TAC Jardinieres are Persian Red 5", Apple Green 7", and the seldom found Burgundy 7" piece. $30-45 for 5" and $60-90 for either 7" piece

Wall Pockets

Wall pocket production at Trenton Potteries commenced during the TEPECO years and increased during the TAC years. Despite being part of the general line of artwares, wall pockets remain difficult to find today, especially in premium colors and with any decoration.

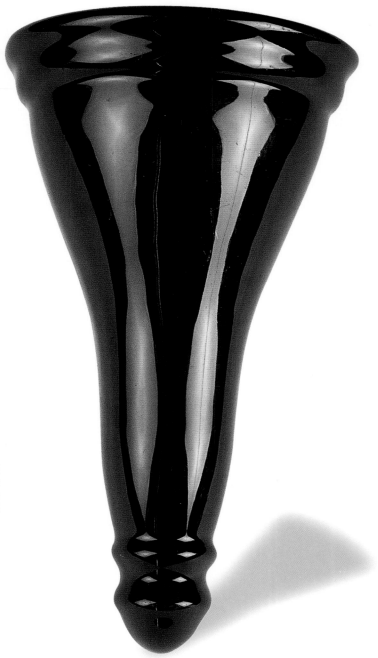

A 9" TEPECO Mirror Black wall pocket in a subtle Deco form. In common colors $75-125, in Mirror Black $125-175

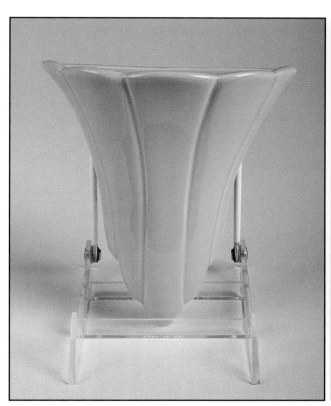

A 6" TAC Spring Yellow #3100 wall pocket. $75-100

This #4100 wall pocket in India Ivory measures 9 1/2" in length by 8" in width. It is found with both TEPECO and TAC marks on it. It resembles two cornucopias joined by a subtle diamond design. $125-175

A simple 6" high x 8" wide TAC wall pocket in Turquoise Blue. $75-125

This 6" high x 8" wide TAC wall pocket with detailed oriental design is both rare and desirable. $350-500 the pair

A detail of the intricate decoration on the wall pockets.

TEPECO Vases, Urns, and Rose Bowls

The origins of the Trenton Potteries Company's venture into the artware and giftware market place are exhibited in this section. Here are examples of the initial shapes and colors that defined TEPECO during the 1932 to 1935 period. Some items shown were experimental or one-of-a-kind. Some of the colors are rarely encountered and may have only been produced for a few months, not years. Due to the lack of company records, some questions remain unanswered.

These miniatures or salesmen's samples have been found with both TEPECO and TAC marks. These 3 1/4"vases are identical to the larger pieces found in the photos on pages 85 and 92. Ivory, Apple Green, and turquoise "minis" are very desirable. $60-90 each

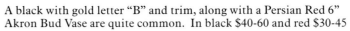
A black with gold letter "B" and trim, along with a Persian Red 6" Akron Bud Vase are quite common. In black $40-60 and red $30-45

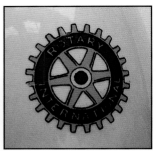

A "Rotary International" decal found on an Akron Bud Vase. *Courtesy Ed Watkinson* $40-60

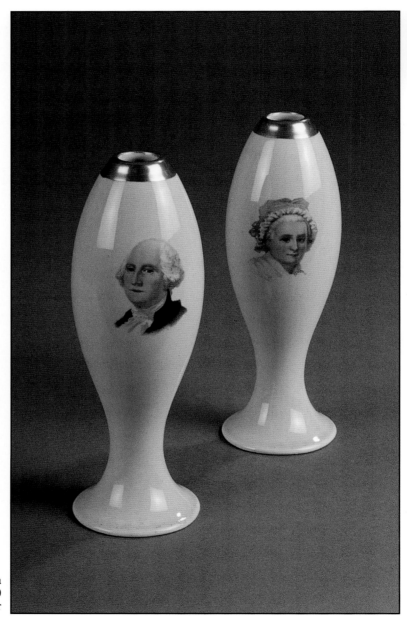

A pair of 6" Akron Bud Vases with matching George and Martha Washington decals with gold trim on an ivory background. $100-150 the pair

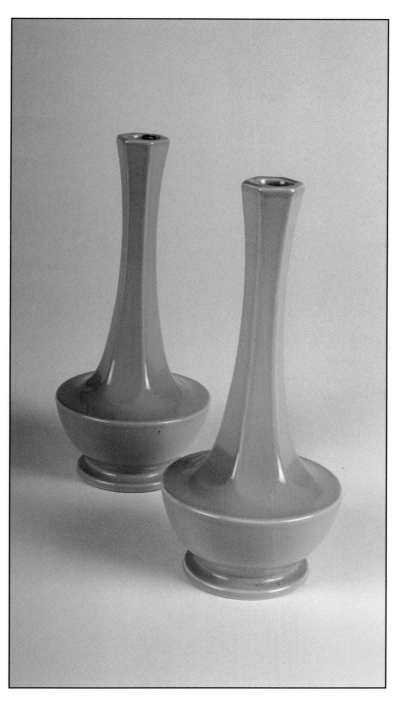

Left: A 7" Aleda Bud Vase in Pale Jade is one of the more uncommon Bud Vases. *Courtesy Joe Ozga* $60-90

Right: A pair of 8" Mayfair bud vases in Pale Jade (front) and Apple Green (back) with very delicate lines leading from the neck to the body of the vase. $50-75 each

Left: Three 8" Laverne Bud Vases in Dark Mottled Brown, Apple Green, and Black glazes. Apple Green $40-60 and for Brown or Black $50-75

Right: Three 7 1/2" bud vases in premium colors are shown in this photo. During the TAC production period this bud vase was given a pair of long handles from the top rim to the bulbous body. This bud vase without handles is much less common. In common colors $50-75. In the colors shown here, Orchid Pink (front), matte medium blue (middle), and Rose (rear) value is $75-125 each

Left: An 8" flaring bud vase in Oxford Blue on left and a 6" Fluted Vase in Turquoise Blue capture the subtle lines that move through these deco objects. 8" vase in common colors $60-90 and in Oxford Blue $75-125. Value for 6" vase $50-75

Right: These two bottle shaped and baluster shaped vases have an aesthetic appeal. The Rose colored 7 1/2" and Oxford Blue 6 1/4" vase are infrequently found. In common colors $60-90 each and in blue or rose $75-125 each

Some of the least commonly found Trenton Potteries colors are shown in this grouping of five Tumbler Vases. TEPECO mentions that the vases measure 7", but the Rose colored vase in the front measures only 6"! From left to right, behind the 6" vase are a Pearl Grey, a pale pink, a Venetian Blue, and a matte sky blue 7" Tumbler Vase. Along with the matte black and Purple vases, the gray, pale pink, and matte sky blue colors are truly rare. 6" vase $75-125. Value for common color 7" Tumbler vases $40-60 each, uncommon colors $60-90 each, and rare colors $100-150 each

This cubist influenced Square Vase measures 8" and has 16 individual panels. The linear proportions to this vase make it one of TEPECO's finest. In common colors $140-200 and in Rose or other premium colors $200-300

A grouping of three TEPECO rose bowls measure 4" high by 7" wide for the Citrus Yellow bowl in front and 6 1/2" high by 7" wide for the Venetian Blue and Pink pieces in the rear. The larger rose bowls were produced during the TAC periods as well, and are common. $40-60 in common colors each, and $60-90 for pink and blue each

Trenton produced a 6" and a 9" Hexagonal Flower Vase. They can still be frequently found in both sizes. 6" in common colors $30-45 and premium colors $50-75. Value for 9" is $50-75 for common, and $75-125 for better colors

Two Hexagonal Flower vases measuring 9" are shown in the rare Fern Green and mirror Black glazes. The color variation between these two pieces is minute. Fern Green $100-150 and Black $75-125

This 9 1/2" Dark Mottled Brown vase is the "Big Brother" to the 3 1/4" salesman's samples seen on page 77. This is an uncommon piece. $160-240 in brown

Probably the most common shape ever produced by T. P. Co. was their #354 Urn. These two medium-sized 8" vases come in an unusual semi-gloss white and common turquoise color. Semi-gloss white $50-75 and in turquoise $35-50

Two-Handle Jug
vases measuring
6 3/4" in two colors.
The mirror Black
and Persian Red
vases resemble a
person with hands on
hips! In common
colors $60-90, and in
Black $75-125

These Greek Vases designed in 1933 by Elisabeth Brown, are 9" tall and quite attractive. The three colors seen in this photo are all premium colors. In front is a matte medium blue, followed by a glossy pink, and finally a semi-gloss white vase. Common colors $75-125 and for premium colors $125-175

Produced in 1932, this 7" 2-handled vase shown in Light Mottled Brown (front) and Dark Brown (rear) is part of the small grouping of vases Trenton introduced to the market place in February 1933. $75-100 in common colors and $100-125 in either brown color

8" two-handled vase in Persian Red is slightly larger and more elegant than the vases on the previous page. The design at the base, the handle lines, and the flowing rim indicate a greater degree of thought and workmanship in this piece. $100-150

Fern Green ring vase stands 10 1/2" tall. In common colors $100-150, in Fern Green $140-200, and the rare matte black $200-300

The Trentonian Vase measuring 12" in Fern Green is identical to the Venetian blue vase on page 24. In common colors $140-200 and in Fern Green $180-275

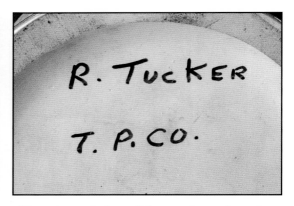

Photo shows the base of the experimental vase in the preceding photo. R. Tucker may have either decorated this vase and/or may have become the proud owner of it. *Courtesy Martin Winar*

Right: This experimental glaze Thistle Vase is a special find. The common gold trim on the rim is complemented by streaks of brown on a yellow background. This style of decorating does not appear in any other pieces the author has ever seen. *Courtesy Martin Winar* is $400-600

Left: The #150 Thistle Vase measuring 15" is a footed, flaring deco vase. This vase was later changed by removing the base. This attractive pair is pictured in Rose and Pale Jade. In common colors $160-240 and in these colors $200-300 each.

12" Standard Vase was one of the early shapes produced by the pottery in the early 1930s. This pale salmon is a seldom seen color. $250-350

This extremely rare and attractive 12" Standard Vase in the expensive marbleized glaze is only one of several known. No two marbleized vases are identical and this piece combines the colors of Lavender, Citrus Yellow, Black, Grey, White, and Persian Red. $750-1000

Left: These 16" Empire Vases in semi-gloss white and mirror black are very strong, decorative pieces. $140-200 in common colors and $200-300 in the pictured colors each.

Right: Extremely rare Cobalt Blue and Citrus Yellow, layered Empire Vase is striking in its 16" of beauty. *Courtesy Martin Winar* $600-900

This 13" Peony Vase must have been the shape used for many experimental and rare glazed pieces. This Venetian Blue glazed vase has the incised numbers 58 5 29 on its underside. There are glaze flaws throughout the vase, but the piece is intriguing and one can only wonder if the 5 29 could refer to that date. $250-350

TEPECO marked 13" Peony Vase glazed in a blended India Ivory and Persian Red combination. While these colors are most common by themselves, this blended look is very rare. $350-500

Richly glazed tricolor blended 13" Peony Vase, predominately ocean blue (Marine Blue?), India Ivory, and Persian Red. It is one of a kind. $600-900

Two 13" Peony Vases with marbleized glazes are featured in this photograph. One of the marks is TEPECO, the other is marked SOLD E. MILLER MAIN OFFICE (See photo below). The subtle colors combine for a mesmerizing image. *Courtesy Martin Winar* $750-1000 each

The underside of rear vase in photo on left is pictured here. It stands to reason that this piece never was marketed to the general public.

A 13" Peony Vase with a CRANE Persian Red glaze which was used from the beginning until the end of pottery production at T. P. Co. It is difficult to ascertain if this was an early glaze sample piece or a close-out piece. $200-300

Trent Art China

Decorated Urns and Vases

During the 1932-1935 TEPECO era of artware production, very little decorating was done. Finding a decal or gold trim was by far the exception rather than the rule. Then, with a new philosophy and new name, Trent Art China (TAC) took the Trenton Potteries in a new direction. Decorating urns and vases became a large part of the total output. Gold decorating firms such as Wheeling and Stouffer were contracted to do some of the gold overlay work for TAC.

As can be seen from the items in this section, the vast majority of gold trimming and decal application took place on Gloss White and India Ivory vases. Also, the majority of the shapes that were decorated were classical; only an occasional Deco shaped item received a decorator's attention.

In determining values for decorated pieces, several factors come into play. First, the common issues such as size and shape are considered. Secondly, the scarcity of the piece is a factor. Finally, with decorated pieces, appearance is very important. It is a pricing consideration when a vase or urn makes an appealing statement!

A common 6" and 8" gold trimmed urn with floral decal and Victorian lovers decal respectively, are shown here. 6" $30-45 and 8" $40-60

Two different gold trimmed 8" urns in white and ivory bodies. With floral decal $40-60, without decal $30-45

An 8" decorated urn with finely painted handles, rim, and base. The large floral decal is accompanied by the signature R. Stuart. Several other pieces have been found bearing this signature. Usually, the quality of these pieces is superior to the common decal items. $75-125

In this photo we find a rare hand-painted 8" Urn with a Mediterranean villa scene, complete with lake, sailboat, and birds. $140-200

A hard to find 12" urn with Victorian lovers scenes and gold trim. *Courtesy Martin Winar* $125-175

The reverse side of the urn in photo #5 depicts a different scene. *Courtesy Martin Winar*

12" urn in ivory depicts and old English tavern scene. This decal is more unusual than those on the left, but here the front and back are identical $125-175

Elegant and colorful pair of 9 3/4" covered urns with floral decals and gold trim. The urn on the left shows the front while the urn on the right depicts the reverse of this matching set. $140-200 the pair

Matching pair of 14 1/2" covered urns illustrating both the obverse and reverse sides of these impressive vitreous china pieces. These floral decorated urns have integral lids as do the 9 3/4" ones on the left. $250-350 the pair

Left: Handsome urn vase measuring 9" has gold trim with a ribbon and bouquet of flowers. $60-90

Right: 9" India Ivory urn vase decorated with Oxford Blue flowers throughout most of the vase. There is less gold trim on this piece than the piece on the left. *Courtesy Martin Winar* $60-90

8" footed classical-shaped Savoy Vase with a gold wreath and torch motif. In June of 1941 the list price for this decorated piece was $7.00, but TAC was offering the trade a 50% discount. $75-100

6" version of an urn vase decorated in a stunning Cobalt Blue, fine gold trim, and very delicate floral design. This piece of vitreous china has the look and feel of fine European porcelain. Due to its color, quality, and unusual size, this vase commands a premium. *Courtesy Joe Ozga* $140-200

Three Bernardo Urns give a sense of classical simplicity. The urn in the front measures 8" and the two in the back 10" each. 8" vase with decal $35-50, 10" with decal $50-75, and 10" Cobalt Blue without decal $60-90

This 10" Bernardo Urn has a fancier gold trimmed decal and gold decoration than the two decorated pieces in the previous photo. *Courtesy Martin Winar* $75-100

Scenic decorated Bernardo 10" Urn has a white background with a Persian Red design as well as the standard gold trim. It is quite unusual. *Courtesy Martin Winar* $100-125

The common 7 1/2" #370 vases. The three gold trimmed Gloss White, Persian Red, and Oxford Blue vases make a patriotic statement. $40-60 for blue, and $35-50 for both the white with decal and the red without decal

7 1/2" vase with a bolder decal than the vase in the previous photo. Furthermore, there is also a small decal at the top of this vase. *Courtesy Martin Winar* $50-75

A very rare version of the 5" Paradise flower holder can be seen in the foreground. In the background is the standard Paradise piece. The floral motif on this unique version is carved as opposed to the berries and leaves that are in relief. The painting on this piece appears to be unfinished or worn. *Courtesy Joe Ozga* $100-150

This 8" four-footed Limoges-style vase is elegant and simultaneously bold. The strong floral decal signed R. Stuart balances against this classical shape. $180-275

This 10" tulip vase is a rare find! While the tulip vases can be found, this is the first professionally painted one the author has ever seen! *Courtesy Joe Ozga* $180-275

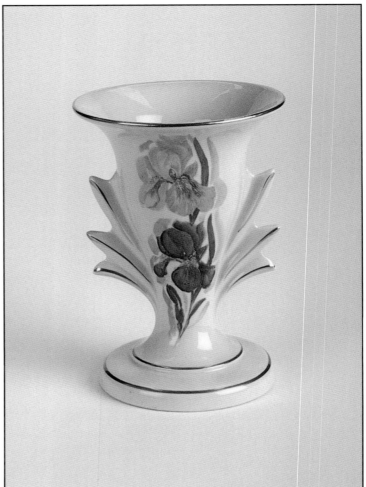

This tastefully decorated 8" vase with protruding handles has a larger decal on front (with two flowers) than on the back (with single flower). A fine example of a decorated TAC vase. *Courtesy Penny Pypcznski* $100-125

12" Acantha Urn with applied floral decal and fine gold trim. $140-200

6" Cameo vase with unusually colorful English cottage scene decal and gold trim, is found on a glossy white background. $60-90

Silver and black outlined 9" Circlet deco vase with a fruit and/or flower decoration, hand-painted on both sides. It is very unusual and it has a distinctive oriental feel to it. $200-300

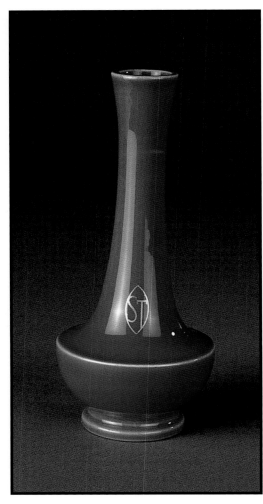

Laverne bud vase in Oxford Blue with the simple gold lettering S T. In all likelihood this piece was in a room at the former Stacy Trent Hotel in Trenton. *Courtesy Martin Winar* $50-75

These two very common 7" Bowl vases in Spring Yellow and Oxford Blue are accentuated with five increasing bands of gold. Yellow $60-90 and blue $75-100

6" Cameo vase decorated by Stouffer Fine China (see page 31) is also signed by A. Rhodes, presumably the decorator. There is a slightly different floral design on each side. $140-200

This detail captures the bright and reflective quality of the gold work done by Stouffer Fine China's decorating department. Note the signature in the lower left hand corner.

Vase with a gold overlay decorated by the Wheeling Decorating Co. of West Virginia. (see page 31) This fine Pickard style finish makes this piece attractive and desirable. $180-275

The same 10" vase shown in the previous photo is now stripped of its gold and instead has become a Bausch and Lomb advertising piece for "Loxit" eye wear that accentuates beauty. The decal is applied to the vase in three sections. $160-240

Undecorated Vases and Urns

During the Trent Art China (TAC) period from 1935 to 1942, some of the finest Deco shaped vitreous chinawares were produced at the Trenton Potteries plant on North Clinton Avenue. Due to changing economic conditions and possible image considerations, new ideas were implemented. The number of glaze colors was scaled back, but decorating vitreous china became popular. Certain TEPECO artware lines were halted, while others were continued. Some vases were modified by adding or deleting parts. TAC production also displayed how subtle linear and geometric variations could impact visual differences among the items.

The full extent of the company's innovations is not yet known, but on the following pages some of the story is unfolded. Decisions and concerted efforts among the industrial designers, laborers, and management brought about the evolution of these artwares.

A Persian Red TAC vase with paper label. The TEPECO version is behind it and is identical except for the handles. TAC vase $40-60

Left: The same red vase but this one is dwarfed by the 16" floor vase in glossy white. 16" vase $250-350

Right: The TEPECO Rose colored 15" Thistle Vase became the 14" vase #390 seen in Turquoise Blue by eliminating the footed base. 14" TAC vase in turquoise $140-200

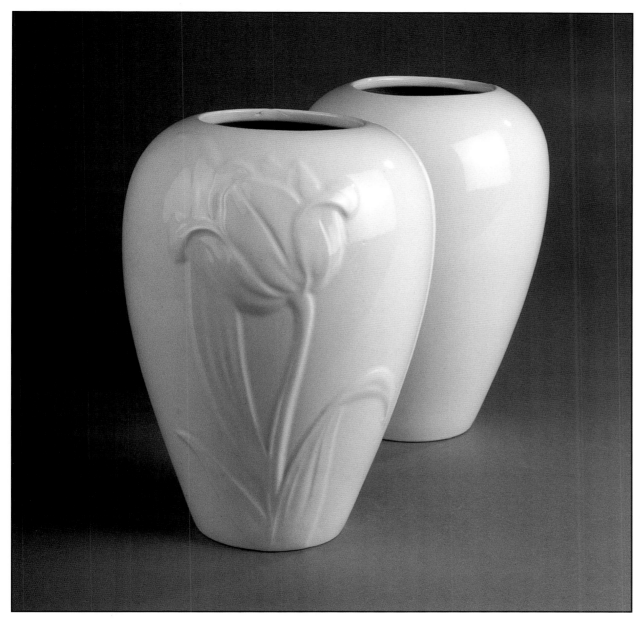

Two 10" TAC vases in Gloss White. The one in front has a tulip motif embossed. Tulip vase $125-175 and plain vase $75-100

The rarely seen 11" Shellburn vase in Oxford Blue is quite a find. The geometric proportions give this a much different appearance than the 6" vases on the next page. *Courtesy Joe Ozga* 11" vase in common colors $200-300 and in Oxford Blue $250-350

The Deco shaped 6" Shellburn Vase is shown in three of the most common TAC colors, Gloss White, Persian Red, and Turquoise Blue. In these colors $75-125 each

A variety of colors make up this display of 6" Circlet vases (also known as Disc vases) which were designed by G. McStay Jackson. White, yellow, red, and turquoise $60-90 each, and pale Apple Green $75-100

All 4 sizes of the Circlet (Disc) vases are shown here. The smallest 6" vase in turquoise is next to the 9" Sky Blue and Gloss White vases. The hard to find 12" vase fronts the extremely difficult to find 16" piece. In common colors for 6" $60-90, 9" $125-175, 12" $250-350, and 16" $600-900. Uncommon to rare colors such as Sky Blue are 6" $100-150, 9" $200-300, 12" $350-500, 16" $1000-1500

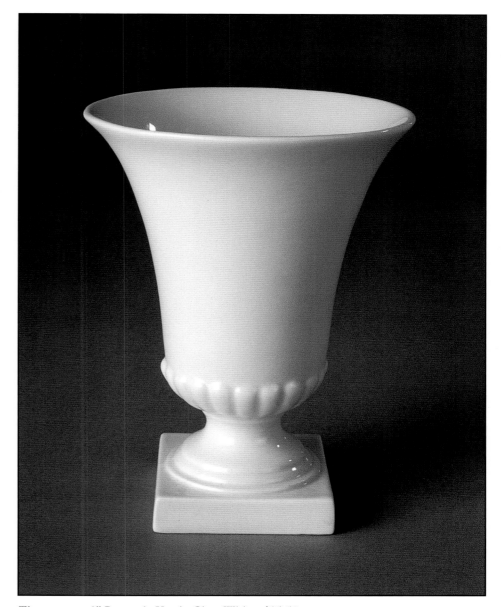

The common 8" Bernardo Urn in Gloss White. $35-50

The Empire Vase was one of the lines that existed during the TEPECO and TAC periods. The Apple Green miniature and India Ivory vases are both marked TAC and measure 3 1/4" and 12" respectively. 3 1/4" vase $60-90 and 12" vase $140-200

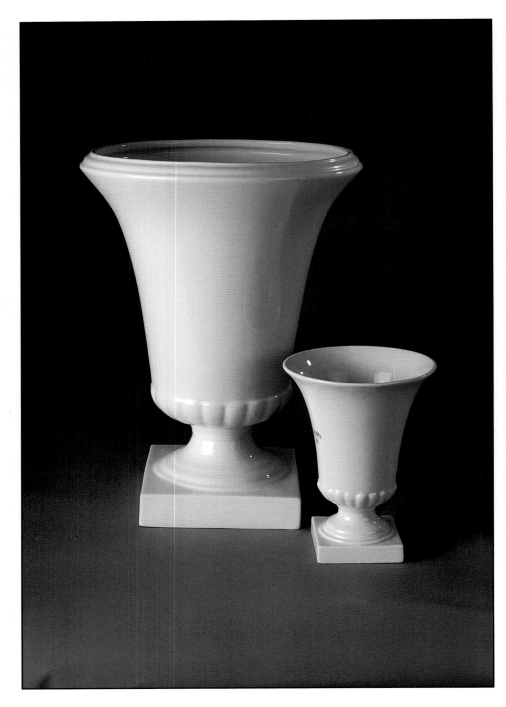

This rare 22" high Bernardo Vase differs in its proportions to the small vase in this line due to its elongated body. The 8", 10", and 16" pieces are more squat in appearance. 22" vase $350-500

The common Bernardo Urn becomes more difficult to find in the larger sizes. Pictured here is the 16" next to the 8" vase. The 16" has a few rings around the top rim area. *Courtesy Martin Winar* 16" $160-240

Two of the 10" Bernardo Urns are shown in proportion to the 22" piece. The Cobalt Blue vase is unfinished and still could use a decal and gold trim. Either 10" urn $60-90

These two TAC marked Turquoise Blue vases are the same shape. The salesmen's sample in the front measures 3 1/4" and the uncommon floor vase measures 12". 3 1/4" vase $60-90 and 12" vase $160-240

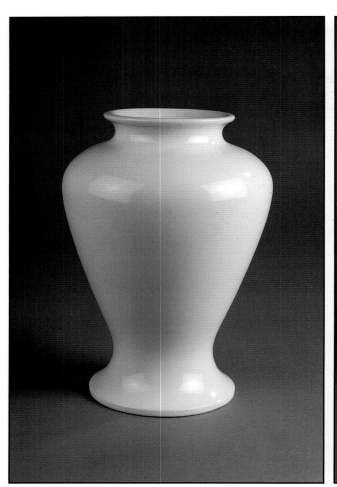

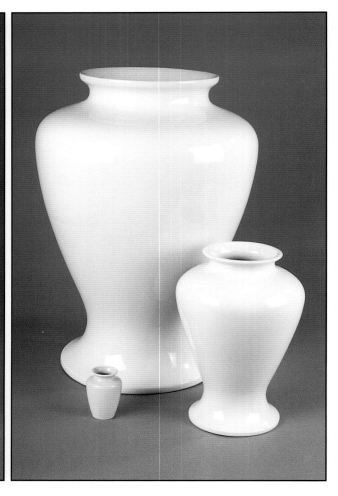

These three pictures tell a story. The first shows the largest overall vitreous china vase made by TEPECO or TAC. It measures 22" in height, but how big is that really? The second view shows the 22" vase next to a 10" vase. The third view shows an additional 3 1/4" salesman's sample to give a sense of how big these pieces really are! 10" vase $100-150, 18" vase (not pictured) $200-300, and 22" vase $400-600

Two of G. McStay Jackson's Orbit vases measuring 6" and 9" respectively. These designs are frequently found and sought after for their Art Deco appeal. 6" in Persian Red $60-90 and 9" in India Ivory $125-175

With only subtle changes, the Orbit vase becomes the 7" Crossley vase. The Crossley Vase is much less frequently seen and is very desirable. 6" Orbit vase $60-90 and the Crossley Vase $140-200

The Crossley family played a prominent role both in the city of Trenton and its ceramics industry. The first Crossley to influence the potteries here was Joseph Crossley, president and owner of Crossley Machine Co. The company, which still exists today, was founded around 1879 and manufactured clay-working machinery. He had contacts with the Trenton Potteries Company, among others.

Joseph Crossley's son, George C. Crossley, was president and owner of the United Clay Mines Corp. and Prospect Street National Bank in Trenton. He provided clay and financial backing to the Trenton Potteries Company and other potteries in the city.

The Crossley Vase is one of TAC's Art Deco successes. It captures the essence of the 1930s with strong lines engulfing the Orbit.

The #300 line of Hexagonal Flower Vases was carried on from the TEPECO to the TAC line. 6" in Oxford Blue $40-60 and 9" in Turquoise Blue $50-75

These two Greek urn vases remained in the Trenton Potteries line from 1932 to its end. 6" white $25-35 and 8" Oxford Blue $50-75

#200 series bud vase in both the TEPECO and TAC lines. These two are marked TAC. $30-45 each

The Argent Urns measure 6" and 8" respectively. The matte dark blue and Cobalt Blue vases are striking and infrequently found. 6" urns in common colors $40-60 and in either blue shown here $60-90. The 8" urn vase in white $60-90

Opposite page:
The 7" bowl vases are marked TAC. They are also found with TEPECO marks (see page 83). White or turquoise $40-60 each, and Fern Green $50-75

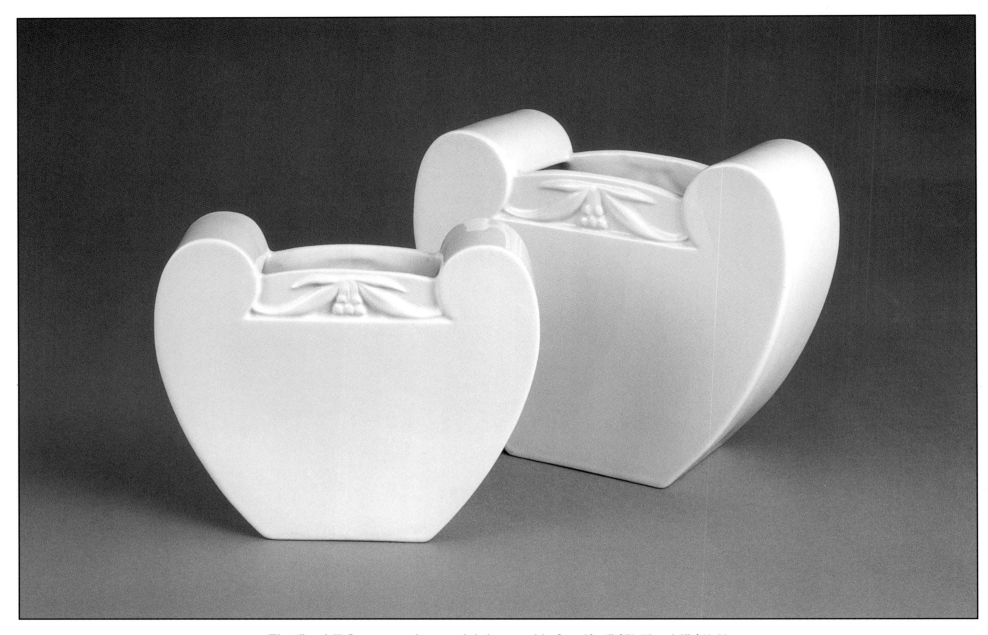

The 6" and 7" Cameo vases have a subtle berry and leaf motif. 6" $50-75 and 7" $60-90

Gloss White TAC planter/vase resembles cylindrical vases in the preceding picture. Measuring 5 1/4" high and 5 1/2" in diameter, it may have been produced in other sizes. *Courtesy Fritz Karch* $125-175

These attractive Art Deco cylindrical vases with repeating vertical bands are infrequently seen and are aesthetically pleasing. The 5" Oxford Blue vase and 9" Turquoise Blue vase compliment each other. 5" in common colors $60-90 and in Oxford Blue $75-125. Value for the 9" vase $160-240

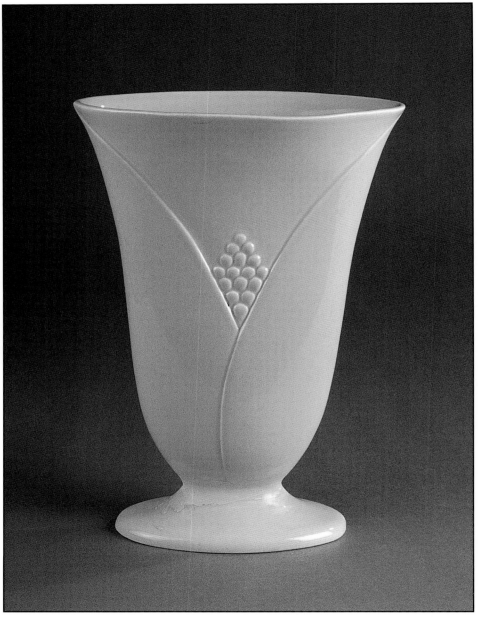

Sleek and elegant 7 1/2" Tyrol Vases in India Ivory and an unglazed bisque finish. The bisque vase shows how white the vitreous clay is in its natural state. 7 1/2" vase $75-100 each

This 12" Tyrol Vase in Spring Yellow is very fragile. A small base and flaring top make this vase susceptible to damage; very few are still found. $200-300

10" vase in bright Spring Yellow subtly flares and gently steps back at the top rim. $140-200

Rare and impressive 14" dark chocolate brown Art Deco vase with a carved horizontal band of berries and leaves. In common colors or dark chocolate brown $300-400

10" Deerwood Vases capture a sense of the Art Deco movement. A side view of the turquoise vase captures the lines of the handles, while the white vase captures the stylized deer and hanging berries motif. $140-200 each in these common colors

Oxford Blue 11 1/2" cylindrical vase with a 2/3" lip in Art Deco design. This is a hard-to-find piece in a desirable color. *Courtesy Fritz Karch* In common colors $180-275, and in Oxford Blue $250-350

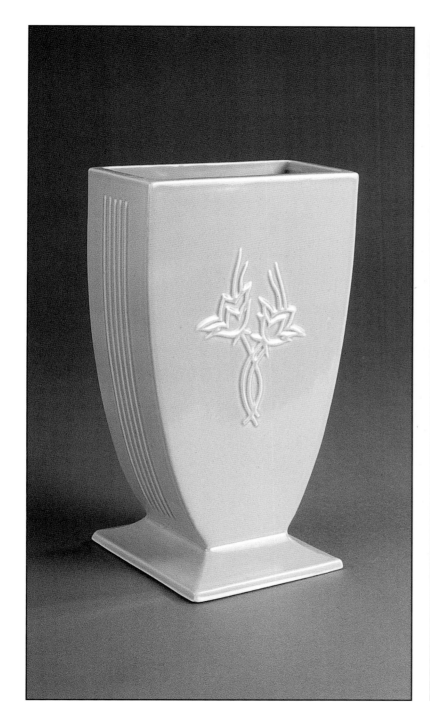

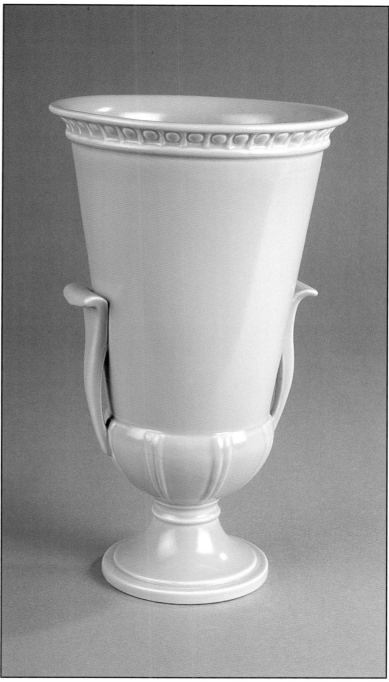

Left: 10 1/2" Iris Vase in chartreuse color. In the front and back are stylized irises and on the sides are thin vertical lines. $125-175

Right: This predominantly classical 13" urn with Art Deco overtones is an impressive piece in this chartreuse color. $160-240

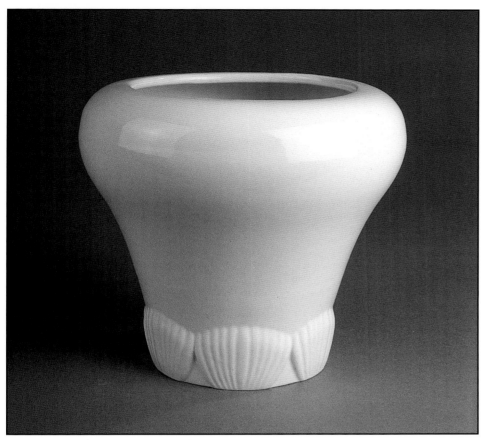

The 8" high Shelton Vase in white is wider than it is tall. The TAC catalog lists this piece as 7" tall, but the vase pictured here is 8" tall. A band of stylized shells trims the base. $125-175

The 12" Acantha Urn is a Classical form with a footed base and gently rounded handles. $125-175

Opposite page
Left: A *Crockery and Glass Journal* issue from February, 1937, listed this 12" vase as a new item with an "Empire feeling." It is not rare, but combines traditional and Deco elements in its form. $140-200

Right: The simple Gloss White 9" TAC vase with an all encompassing wreath motif. *Courtesy Martin Winar* $125-175

The 8" Iliad Vase in Persian Red is a masterpiece in symmetry. This side has "V" shaped steps. *Courtesy Joe Ozga* $200-300

The other side of the 8" Iliad Vase has a subtle angular plane that covers more than half of the side.

This Spring Yellow Epergne, measuring 10" in diameter and 6 1/2" in height, has two levels for displaying flowers and other decorative items. The G. McStay Jackson design also has been referred to as a "Bacchanale". $100-150

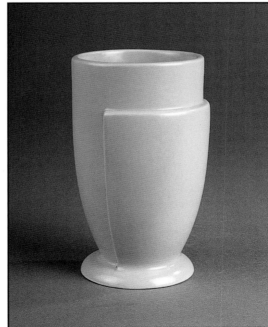

This 7 1/2" Choral Vase has strong Deco lines and is bold in the common Apple Green color. $100-125

136

Two 5 3/4" Deco vases in Apple Green and Persian Red seen from different angles. $60-90 each.

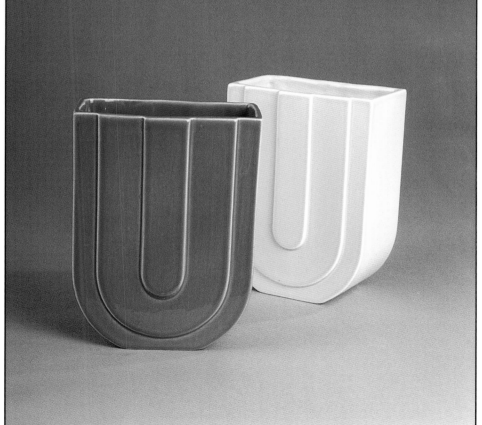

Art Deco 7 1/2" Mayfair Vases in Oxford Blue and Spring Yellow. Note that there are three distinct surfaces, most evident on the yellow vase. Yellow $75-125 and blue $100-150

The Delphi Vase, measuring 8", is a combination of traditional and Deco lines. This Persian Red vase has a TAC ink stamp and an American Trent Art China paper label. $75-125

A green 7" Flute vase of limited availability $100-125

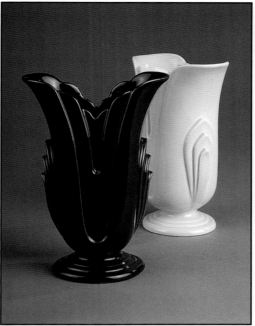

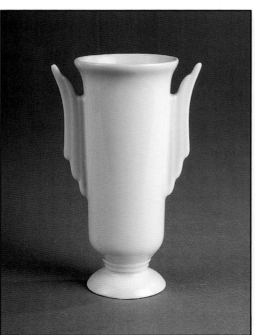
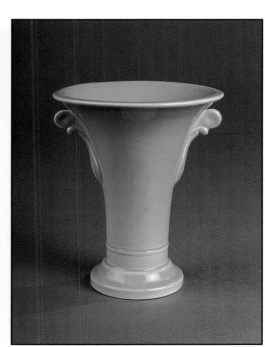

Top left: 7" Turquoise Blue bud vase is not common. It has a wider neck and body than most TEPECO or TAC bud vases. The simple lines around the body are distinctly Deco. $100-125

Bottom left: 7" TAC Thistle Vase is not to be mistaken for the 15" TEPECO "Thistle" vase (see pages 90 and 114). $75-125

Top center: Flaring 8" vases with various surface levels. The multi-dimensional nature of this vase is strikingly apparent on the Cobalt Blue one. $125-175 for Cobalt Blue and $75-100 for Ivory

Bottom center: 6 1/2" white TAC winged vase is delicate, fragile, and uncommon. $75-100

Top right: One of TAC's more unusual examples, this 8" vase is susceptible to damage due to its protruding handles. Its appeal lies in its atypical form. $75-125

Bottom right: Flaring 7 1/2" Turquoise Blue vase with similar, but not identical, handles to the 9" vase on the next page, lower left. $75-100

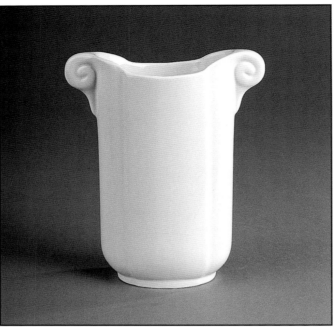

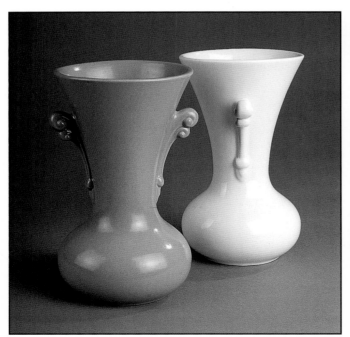

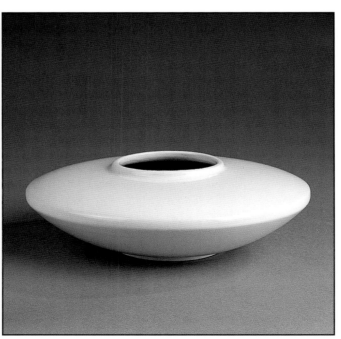

Top left: These 7" Rhythm Vases can really make some noise when you get a grouping together! They are fairly common, but their striking Art Deco appeal is apparent. Dark matte blue $125-175 and Turquoise Blue $75-100

Bottom left: 9" high curled handle vases in Fern Green and Gloss White. Frontal and side views of this vase give a sense of the proportion of the vase and its handles. In Fern Green $100-150 and in white $75-100

Top right: 7 1/2" curled handle vase that is very simple in its design. $60-90

Bottom right: One of designer G. McStay Jackson's Deco delights! Promoted as the Flower Dial in the mid- to late 1930s, it is commonly referred to as the "Flying Saucer" vase today. This flower holder has refreshingly clean lines and is sought after by collectors. 10" flying saucer vase $125-175

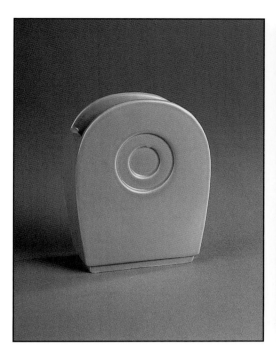
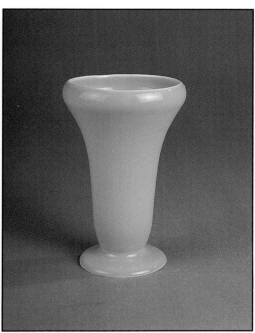
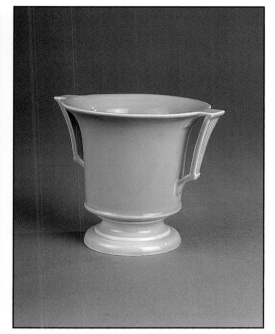

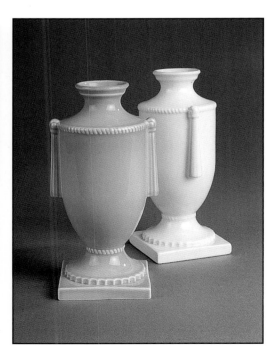

Top left: The 6" Caprice vase with recessed rings is a quintessential Art Deco design. The Fern Green color is not common on this vase. In common colors $60-90 and in Fern Green $100-125

Bottom left: 5 3/4" chartreuse vase with subtle vertical lines extending from the top rim to the foot. $50-75 in chartreuse and common colors

Top center: This 7 3/4" flaring chalice vase in turquoise has Art Deco style. $60-90

Bottom center: 9" Turquoise Tempo Vase, like the preceding chalice vase, is basic in its design and functional without flare. It is more common than the chalice vase. $60-90

Top right: Turquoise Blue glaze adorns this 5 1/2" urn vase. Note the detail of vertical lines on the handles. $50-75

Bottom right: The two urns are identical to the urns on page 100 except that the decorated urns had integral lids. These urns had removable lids which, after 65 years, are missing; this is more the rule than the exception. Common colors without lid 8" tall $50-75 each, and common colors with lid 9 3/4" tall $75-100 each

The 8" Savoy Vase in Persian Red has a Classical shape. The identical piece with a gold wreath and torch design can be seen on page 102. 8" vase $50-75

9" urn vase in India Ivory. $50-75

The 6" Shell vase in India Ivory is a common vase in a common color. For the beginning collector who wants different colors, this is a fun and inexpensive shape to find. Shell vases in different colors are attractive when placed together on a shelf and are nice decorative pieces in a shore house. India Ivory and common colors $35-50, uncommon to rare colors $50-75 each

Brochure and 1941 Pricing

A 22-page, undated, American Trent Art China brochure from the late 1930s or possibly early 1940s is shown along with a four-page price list dated June 1, 1941. The brochure contains important information concerning the original names of artware lines, their sizes, and model numbers. Other insight gathered from this catalogue reveals the company's statements regarding quality and their intent to design vessels to "harmonize with period and contemporary furnishings."

The price list includes information concerning colors, gold trimmings, floral decals, in-stock items, and availability, as well as the original retail prices. Also, this is one of the latest dated TAC documents. The last mention of TAC artwares are found in ceramic trade materials from 1942.

The following information was made possible from the collaborative efforts of Mr. Ed Watkinson and his grandmother, the late Verena B. Wilson.

Flower arrangement by Mrs. J. McStay Jackson, Chicago, Ill.

Beautiful Flowers
Merit Beautiful Settings

CREATED as the finishing touch of nature's beauty, flowers afford us unlimited possibilities in beautifying our homes and surroundings. The beauty they afford us, however, can never be realized to the best advantage by simply stuffing them in the first receptacle that comes to hand with but scant consideration for the design and color harmony of the entire composition. Regardless of their inherent beauty, cut flowers are only at their best when artistically arranged in appropriate containers that enhance their natural loveliness, and we owe it to nature to place them only in vases or bowls that are carefully selected to afford them the most attractive setting.

No. 351 BOWL, 9 inches Diameter
No. 353 CANDLE HOLDER

Flowers above and below arranged by Miss Frances Jones, Cincinnati, Ohio

No. 7006 CANDLE HOLDER   No. 7001 BOWL, 9¼ inches Diameter   No. 7006 CANDLE HOLDER

No. 530 BOWL, 11½ inches Diameter
No. 532 CANDLE HOLDER

No. 9044 BOWL, 12½ inches Long
No. 9051 CANDLE HOLDERS

Flowers arranged by Mrs. J. McStay Jackson, Chicago, Ill.

No. 522
CANDLE HOLDER   No. 520 BOWL
10 inches Diameter   No. 522
CANDLE HOLDER

No. 516 BOWL, 12 inches Long
No. 518 CANDLE HOLDERS

No. 9003 FANTASY
13 inches x 4½ inches

No. 9010
CANDLE STICK

No. 9008 GONDOLA
12 x 4½ inches

No. 9010
CANDLE STICK

No. 9007 LOTUS BOWL
10 inches Diameter

No. 9001 EPERGNE
10 inches Diameter

No. 9037 FLOWER SHELLS and 9038 CANDLE BLOCK
Shells 10 inches x 8¾ inches.   Overall of above 10 inches x 18½ inches

No. 9005 FLOWER DIAL
10 inches Diameter

No. 203 URN
13 inches high

No. 9015 URN
12 inches high

No. 120 ACANTHA URN
12 inches high

{ Page 6 }

No. 170 EMPIRE VASE
16 inches high
12 inches high

No. 202 VASE
14 inches high
9 inches high

{ Page 7 }

146

No. 370 VASE
7½ inches high
16 inches high

No. 1510 VASE
7½ inches high

No. 354 URN
6 inches high
8 inches high
12 inches high

No. 107 BERNARDO URN
8 inches high   10 inches high
16 inches high   22 inches high

No. 125 SAVOY VASE
8 inches high   16 inches high

No. 395 VASE
9 inches high

No. 9025 VASE
7½ inches high

No. 10 VASE
10 inches high
18 inches high   22 inches high

No. 390 VASE
14 inches high

No. 3025 BOWL
7 inches high

No. 1610 VASE
10 inches high

No. 9004 CIRCLET

Arrangement by
MRS. FREDERICK W. LEWIS
Little Neck, Long Island

Awarded First Prize
International Flower Show, New York City

Acclaimed in "The World of Today"
As modern as "The World of Tomorrow"

POSSESSING all the traditional concepts of good design, the harmonious rhythm of related lines combining the nicely balanced proportions of vase and contents distinguish the arrangement to the left as an outstanding achievement in originality and individuality of expression that is characteristic of the modern trend in the art of arranging flowers.

Inspired by the charming simplicity of contemporary styling, this creation of beauty in "The World of Today" demonstrates the trend toward greater originality and beauty in flower arrangements for "The World of Tomorrow."

{ Page 12 }

No. 9011 CIRCLET
6 inches high

No. 9017 CAPRICE
6 inches high

No. 9032 CROSSLY VASE
7 inches high

No. 9004 CIRCLET ARRANGEMENT
by Mrs. Frederick W. Lewis, Little Neck, Long Island

No. 9004 CIRCLET
9 inches diameter
12 inches diameter   16 inches diameter

No. 9002 ORBIT
9 inches diameter

{ Page 13 }

No. 9022 CHORAL VASE
7½ inches high

No. 9002 ORBIT
6 inches high

FLOWER ARRANGEMENTS
by Mrs. McStay Jackson, Chicago, Illinois

No. 9023 RHYTHM VASE
7 inches high

No. 9020 MAYFAIR VASE
7½ inches high

No. 9013 VASE
10 inches high

No. 9047 CAMEO
6 inches high   7 inches high

No. 402 VASE, 9 inches high

No. 9054 DELPHI VASE, 8 inches high
Flowers arranged by
Miss Frances Jones, Cincinnati, Ohio

No. 9039 TYROL VASE
7½ inches high   12 inches high

{ Page 14 }

No. 4100 WALL POCKET
8 inches wide

No. 9036 DEERWOOD VASE, 10 inches high

No. 9052 SHELTON VASE, 7 inches high
Flowers arranged by
Miss Frances Jones, Cincinnati, Ohio

No. 9006 IRIS VASE
10½ inches high

{ Page 15 }

No. 9033 VERDE
4 inches high

No. 9050 PARADISE
5 inches high

No. 9049 ARGENT URN
6 inches high   8 inches high
2.00

No. 4025 SHELL
6 inches high

No. 212 CORNUCOPIA, 5½ inches high

No. 4005 CORNUCOPIA, 6 inches high
Flowers arranged by
Miss Frances Jones, Cincinnati, Ohio

No. 506 RIDGEMORE VASE
6 inches high

No. 9029 TWIRL
6¼ inches long, 3 inches high

No. 200 BUD VASE
8 inches high

No. 3100 WALL POCKET, 6 inches high
Flowers arranged by
Miss Frances Jones, Cincinnati, Ohio

No. 3005 IVY BOWL
7 inches long, No. 3006 10 inches long

No. 9040 CORINTH URN
8 inches high

No. 9043 THISTLE VASE
7 inches high

No. 9019 TEMPO VASE
9 inches high

No. 9048 ILIAD VASE
8 inches high

No. 9041 FLUTE
7 inches high

No. 503 SHELLBURN VASE
11 inches high, No. 502 6 inches high

No. 357 SQUARE POT
4 inches square
5 inches square
6 inches square
7 inches square
8 inches square

No. 5000 POT with integral saucer
7 inches high

No. 355 POT AND SAUCER

| 3 inches high | 4 inches high | 5 inches high |
| 6 inches high | 7 inches high | 9 inches high |

No. 9055 FLOWER BOX
13 inches long, 4½ inches high

No. 5925 JARDINIER
5 inches high, 7 inches high

No. 38 BOWL, 12 inches long

American Trent Art China sets a new standard of beauty in the decorative appointments for the home. Designed especially to accentuate the beauty of flowers and correctly styled to harmonize with period and contemporary furnishings they lend a touch of elegance that enhances the appearance of any interior.

Vastly superior to ordinary pottery, American Trent Art China is genuine china, the same as the finest table china. Beneath the brilliant sheen and colorful surface of a non-absorbent glaze, its hard, impervious body lends it unusual strength and durability. Glazed both inside and outside, American Trent Art China is absolutely impervious, easy to keep clean and is guaranteed not to seep water, craze, stain or discolor.

Every design is stocked in various colors, which have been carefully developed to insure a harmonious blending of these accessories with various flowers and the most popular color schemes of today.

THE TRENTON POTTERIES CO.
TRENTON, N. J., U.S.A.

THE PRIDE OF ARTISTS AND CRAFTSMEN

*C*ENTURIES ago the art of pottery making fell into ill-repute at the hands of unscrupulous Roman potters who deceived the public by concealing, with wax, flaws in their ware which came defective from the firing. To counteract this stigma of suspicion and regain the confidence they deserved, honest potters distinguished their product by marking each piece of ware with the words "*Sine Cera*"—"without wax"—from which is derived the word "sincere," and as further evidence of their sincerity, branded it with their signature.

And thus, reputable potters acquired a means of expressing their pride of workmanship by identifying their product with the individual insignia of the maker. On through the ages, Stradivarius, Rembrandt—all old masters of craft and brush—have practiced and endorsed this custom by registering similar identifications of their efforts.

So today, as for years past, we identify our ware by indelibly stamping every piece with the above trade mark, that those who buy it may be assured of pottery guaranteed by a manufacturer who sells no seconds or culls, and assumes full responsibility for the quality of their product.

THE TRENTON POTTERIES CO.
TRENTON, N. J.

AMERICAN TRENT ART CHINA

June 1, 1941

TRADE DISCOUNT 50%

GENERAL INFORMATION

Effective on the above date, the prices and basis of sales listed herein supersede all previous lists. All design numbers and colors that do not appear in this list have been discontinued and are no longer available.

PRICES

All prices are F.O.B. Trenton, N.J. and apply uniformily to all colors in which the various items are carried in stock. Items which are only carried in stock in white-such as flower pots-can be furnished in color at an additional charge and are listed accordingly.

Prices include packing. Initial orders must total $15.00 net or more. C.O.D. orders only accepted if accompanied with deposit of 20% of amount ordered.

All prices are subject to change without notice. To avoid possible misunderstanding all orders should list prices for everything called for.

CHOICE OF COLORS

Every design with the exception of flower pots is carried in stock in the following colors.

India Ivory........No. 405	Gloss White...........No. 680
Persian Red........No. 485	Turquoise Blue........No. 682
Cobalt Blue........No. 550	Spring Yellow.........No. 689

Twilight Green...No. 719

CLAIMS

All goods are inspected and packed by experienced men. Every precaution is taken against breakage and other damage. Our responsibility, therefore, ceases upon delivery of goods in good condition to the carrier.

DELIVERY

We maintain sufficient stock of the above colors and decorated ware to make shipment of the average run of orders within four days after receipt of same.

A sufficient stock of biscuit is also maintained for replenishing gloss stock in quickest possible time. This minimizes delay in filling orders whenever a sudden increase of sales for any item or particular color exceeds our stock of gloss ware. When this occurs, it requires two weeks to glaze and fire ware before shipment can be made.

PRICE LIST OF ART WARE IN ANY OF ABOVE COLORS
F.O.B. Trenton, N.J.

DESIGN NUMBER	DESCRIPTION and SIZE	UNIT PRICE	DESIGN NUMBER	DESCRIPTION and SIZE	UNIT PRICE
10	Vase, 12 inches high	4.00	354	Urn, 6 inches high	1.50
107	Urn, 8 inches high	2.00	354	Urn, 8 inches high	3.00
107	Urn, 9¾ inches high	3.50	354	Urn, 12 inches high	6.00
107	Urn, 16 inches high	7.50	355	Flower Pot-See Under Flower Pots	
120	Urn, 12 inches high	5.00	357	Flower Pot-See Under Flower Pots	
125	Urn, 8 inches high	3.00	370	Vase, 7½ inches high	1.50
170	Vase, 12 inches high	3.00	390	Vase, 14 inches high	4.00
200	Vase, 8 inches high	1.00	395	Vase, 9 inches high	3.00
202	Vase, 9 inches high	3.00	502	Vase, 6 inches high	1.00
202	Vase, 14 inches high	6.00	506	Vase, 6 inches high	1.00
203	Urn, 13 inches high	6.00	512	Vase, 6 inches high	1.00
212	Cornucopia	1.50	514	Vase, 7½ inches high	1.50
351	Bowl, 9 inches diam.	2.00	516	Bowl, 12 inches long	3.00
353	Candle Holders, in pairs	1.50	518	Candle Holders, in pairs	1.50

DESIGN NUMBER	DESCRIPTION and SIZE	UNIT PRICE	DESIGN NUMBER	DESCRIPTION and SIZE	UNIT PRICE
520	Flower Bowl,10 inches diam.	3.00	9019	Vase, 9 inches high	2.00
522	Candle Holders, in pairs	1.50	9020	Vase, 7½ inches high	2.00
530	Flower Bowl, 11½ inches diam.	3.50	9022	Vase, 7½ inches high	1.50
532	Candle Holder, in pairs	1.50	9023	Vase, 7 inches high	1.00
550	Urn with Cap. 9½ inches high	2.50	9025	Vase, 7½ inches high	1.50
1000	Cornucopia, 9 inches high	3.00	9029	Twirl, 6¾x4½ inches	1.50
1510	Vase, 7½ inches high	2.00	9032	Vase, 7 inches high	3.00
1610	Vase, 10 inches high	3.00	9033	Cornucopia, 4 inches high	1.00
3005	Ivy Bowl, 7 inches long	1.00	9036	Vase, 9¾ inches high	3.00
3006	Ivy Bowl, 10 inches long	2.00	9037	Flower Shell, 10x8¾ inches	3.00
3025	Bowl, 7 inches high	2.00	9038	Candle Block	1.00
3100	Wall Pocket 6 inches high	1.00	9039	Vase, 7½ inches high	1.50
4005	Cornucopia, 6 inches high	1.00	9039	Vase, 12 inches high	4.00
4025	Shell, 6 inches high	1.00	9040	Urn, 8 inches high	2.00
4100	Wall Pocket, 8 inches wide	3.00	9041	Vase, 7 inches high	1.50
5000	Flower Pot-See under Flower Pots		9043	Vase, 7 inches high	1.50
5925	Jardiniere, 5 inches high	1.50	9044	Flower Boat, 12½x5¾ inches	3.50
5925	Jardiniere, 7 inches high	2.00	9047	Cameo, 6 inches high	1.50
7001	Bowl, 9½ inches diam.	2.00	9047	Cameo, 7 inches high	2.00
7006	Candle Holders, in pairs	1.50	9049	Urn, 6 inches high	1.00
9001	Epergne, 10 inches diam.	3.50	9049	Urn, 8 inches high	2.00
9002	Orbit, 6 inches diam.	1.00	9050	Paradise, 5 inches high	1.20
9002	Orbit, 9 inches diam.	3.00	9051	Candle Boats, in pairs	1.50
9003	Fantasay, 13x4½ inches	3.50	9052	Vase, 7 inches high	2.50
9004	Circlet, 9 inches diam.	2.50	9054	Vase, 8 inches high	2.00
9004	Circlet, 12 inches diam.	4.00	9055	Flower Box, 13 inches long	3.00
9005	Flower Dial, 10 inches diam.	3.00	9060	Flower Tray, 10x7¼ inches	3.00
9006	Vase, 10 inches high	3.00	9066	Vase, 8 inches high	2.00
9007	Flower Bowl, 10 inches	3.00	9072	Vase, 6 inches diameter	1.50
9008	Gondola, 12x4½ inches	3.00	9073	Vase, 9 inches high	2.50
9010	Candle Sticks, in pairs	2.00	9077	Wall Vase, 6 inches high	2.00
9011	Circlet, 6 inches diam.	1.00	9078	Urn, 5½ inches high	2.00
9015	Urn, 12 inches high	5.00	9081	Vase, 9 inches high	2.50
9017	Vase, 6 inches high	1.00	170	Vase, 16 inches high	6.00

PRICE LIST OF SMOKERS' ACCESSORIES IN THE FOLLOWING COLORS

White, Turquoise, Ivory, Yellow, Black, Tan, Cobalt, Red.
Cover and bowl of humidor can be furnished in any combination of above colors. The cover is also available in Chocolate Brown.

6150	Humidor, 7 inches diam.	3.00	6425	Ash Tray, 6 inches square	2.50
6412	Ash Tray, 5½ inches daim.	.80			

PRICE LIST OF FLOWER POTS

Flower pots are only carried in stock in white

Colored Flower Pots Take an Extra Charge as Listed and Require Three Weeks for Delivery

No. 355 POTS ONLY WITHOUT DRAIN HOLE

SIZE		PRICE LIST WHITE	COLOR
3"	Pot only	.50	.60
4"	Pot only	.70	.80
5"	Pot only	.80	1.00
6"	Pot only	1.00	1.20
7"	Pot only	1.20	1.50
9"	Pot only	2.00	2.50

No. 357 SQUARE FLOWER POT

SIZE		WHITE	COLOR
4"	Pot	1.00	1.20
5"	Pot	1.40	1.60
6"	Pot	1.80	2.00
7"	Pot	2.00	2.40
8"	Pot	2.50	3.00

No. 355 POTS WITH DRAIN HOLE AND SAUCERS

SIZE		PRICE LIST WHITE	COLOR
3"	Pot and Saucer	.60	.80
4"	Pot and Saucer	.80	1.00
5"	Pot and Saucer	1.00	1.30
6"	Pot and Saucer	1.20	1.50
7"	Pot and Saucer	1.50	2.00
9"	Pot and Saucer	2.40	3.00

No. 5000 POT WITH INTEGRAL SAUCER

SIZE		WHITE	COLOR
7"	Pot	1.50	2.00

PRICE LIST OF DECORATED WARE

WHITE WARE WITH GOLD TRIMMING and FLORAL DECALS

DESIGN NUMBER	DESCRIPTION and SIZE	UNIT PRICE
107	Urn, 8 inches high	4.50
107	Urn, 9¾ inches high	7.00
120	Urn, 12 inches high	9.50
125	Urn, 8 inches high	6.00
170	Vase, 12 inches high	7.00
354	Urn, 6 inches high	4.00
354	Urn, 8 inches high	5.00
354	Urn, 12 inches high	9.50
370	Vase, 7½ inches high	4.00
1510	Vase, 7½ inches high	5.00
5925	Jardiniere, 5 inches high	4.00
5925	Jardiniere, 7 inches high	5.00
9077	Wall Vase, 6 inches high	4.00
9078	Urn, 5½ inches high	4.00
9081	Vase, 9 inches high	5.00
9150	Paradise, 5 inches high	4.00
9177	Wall Pocket, 6 inches high	4.00

IVORY WARE WITH GOLD TRIMMING AND FLORAL DECALS

DESIGN NUMBER	DESCRIPTION and SIZE	UNIT PRICE
354	Urn, 6 inches high	4.00
354	Urn, 8 inches high	5.00
9081	Vase, 9 inches high	5.00

IVORY WARE WITH GOLD TRIMMING AND WATTEAU DECALS

DESIGN NUMBER	DESCRIPTION and SIZE	UNIT PRICE
107	Urn, 9¾ inches high	7.50
354	Urn, 6 inches high	4.50
354	Urn, 8 inches high	6.00
354	Urn, 12 inches high	10.00

WHITE FLOWER POTS WITH GOLD AND FLORAL DECALS

DESIGN NUMBER	DESCRIPTION	UNIT PRICE
355	5" Pot only	2.70
355	6" Pot only	3.30
355	7" Pot only	3.90
355	9" Pot only	5.80

PRICE LIST OF DECORATED WARE

WHITE AND COLORED WARE WITH GOLD DECORATION ONLY

Colors Carried In Stock With Gold Only

DESIGN NUMBER	DESCRIPTION	IVORY	BLACK	RED	COBALT	WHITE	YELLOW	GREEN	UNIT PRICE
107	Urn, 8 inches high	S		S	S	S	S	S	4.50
107	Urn, 10 inches high	S	S	S	S	S	S	S	7.00
120	Urn, 12 inches high	S		S	S	S	S	S	9.50
354	Urn, 6 inches high	S	S	S	S	S	S	S	4.00
354	Urn, 8 inches high	S	S	S	S	S	S	S	5.00
354	Urn, 12 inches high	S	S	S	S	S	S	S	9.50
370	Vase, 7½ inches high	S		S	S	S	S	S	4.00
1510	Vase, 7½ inches high	S		S	S	S	S	S	5.00
5925	Jardiniere, 5" high	S		S	S	S	S	S	4.00
5925	Jardiniere, 7" high	S		S	S	S	S	S	5.00
9077	Wall Vase, 6" high	S		S	S	S	S	S	4.00
9078	Urn, 5½ inches high	S		S	S	S	S	S	4.00

WHITE AND COLORED WARE WITH GOLD LAUREL AND GOLD WREATHS

Colors Carried In Stock With Gold Laurel Dec.

DESIGN NUMBER	DESCRIPTION	IVORY	BLACK	RED	COBALT	WHITE	YELLOW	GREEN	UNIT PRICE
125	Urn, 8 inches high	S		S	S		S	S	7.00
354	Urn, 8 inches high	S	S	S	S	S	S	S	7.50
354	Urn, 12 inches high	S	S	S	S	S	S	S	12.00
9044	Boat, 12½ inches long	S		S	S		S	S	8.50

HAWTHORN CLUSTER ALL OVER DECORATION IN GOLD

DESIGN NUMBER	DESCRIPTION AND DECORATION		UNIT PRICE
125	Urn, 8 inches high	Cobalt or Red with Hawthorn Cluster In Gold	7.00
1610	Vase, 10 inches high	Cobalt or Red with Hawthorn Cluster In Gold	5.50
3025	Vase, 7 inches high	Cobalt or Red with Hawthorn Cluster In Gold	4.00
5925	Jardiniere, 5 inches high	Cobalt or Red with Hawthorn Cluster In Gold	4.50
5925	Jardiniere, 7 inches high	Cobalt or Red with Hawthorn Cluster In Gold	7.50
9081	Vase, 9 inches high	Cobalt or Red with Hawthorn Cluster In Gold	7.00

HAWTHORN CLUSTER ALL OVER DECORATION IN MAROON

DESIGN NUMBER	DESCRIPTION AND DECORATION		UNIT PRICE
125	Urn, 8 inches high	Ivory with Hawthorn Cluster In Maroon	6.00
1610	Vase, 10 inches high	Ivory with Hawthorn Cluster In Maroon	4.50
3025	Vase, 7 inches high	Ivory with Hawthorn Cluster In Maroon	3.50
5925	Jardiniere, 5 inches high	Ivory with Hawthorn Cluster In Maroon	4.00
5925	Jardiniere, 7 inches high	Ivory with Hawthorn Cluster In Maroon	6.50
9081	Vase, 9 inches high	Ivory with Hawthorn Cluster In Maroon	6.00

GOLD TRIM LINE DECORATIONS

DESIGN NUMBER	DESCRIPTION AND DECORATION		UNIT PRICE
351	Bowl, 9 inches diam.	Gold Lines on Ivory, Red, Cobalt, Yellow, Green	5.00
353	Candle Holders	Gold Lines on Ivory, Red, Cobalt, Yellow, Green	4.50 Pr.

Miscellaneous Trenton Potteries Items

A few unusual TEPECO and TAC items not fitting any particular category are pictured here.

Two TEPECO salesmen's samples with TEPECO logos and lettering: BE SURE THIS TRADE MARK IS ON YOUR PLUMBING FIXTURES. One is a bathtub, 5" long x 1 1/2" high, and the other one is a block with 3 holes, 6" long x 1 1/4" high. *Courtesy Joe Ozga* $75-125 each

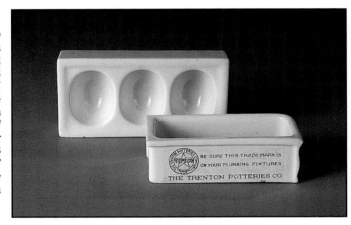

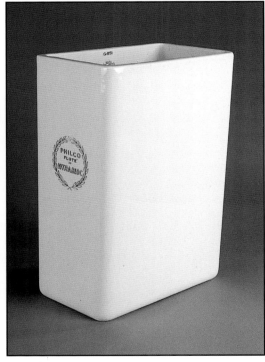

A 15 1/2" Battery Casing with the following lettering: PHILCO Flote in VITRABLOC. The TEPECO mark #1. $100-300

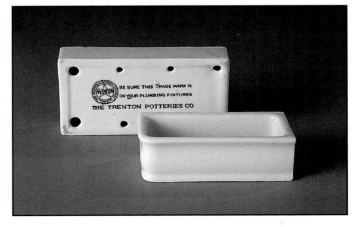

The reverse sides.

An unusual serving or hostess tray in Citrus Yellow bears the TAC mark. It measures 7 3/4" in diameter and 1 3/4" in height. $75-100

Top left: A four-sided, scalloped TAC bowl in Gloss White measuring 3" high and 6" in diameter. *Courtesy Fritz Karch* $50-75

Bottom left: Dark Chocolate Brown bean pot or cookie jar with TEPECO mark is missing its lid. It measures 10" in diameter and is 6 1/2" high without the lid. As found $50-75

Top right: A handsome TEPECO Venetian Blue cookie jar with lid (bean pot) measures 8 1/2" in height. This is indeed a rare piece in this color with a lid. The author has yet to see any other style of cookie jar made by TEPECO or TAC. *Courtesy Martin Winar.* In common colors $125-175 and in Venetian Blue $140-200

Bottom right: This TEPECO bird or chicken feeder ? in glossy white is an unusual shape. It measures 5" in height by 4" in width. *Courtesy Ed Watkinson* Only one ever see; value not determined.

A 6 1/4" elephant planter in an off-white glaze. Is it a Trenton Potteries piece? The planter and its TEPECO mark are puzzling. While no other such mark has been seen on any TEPECO or TAC items, it would also seem implausible that such an item is being forged. The color of the glaze is neither the TEPECO Gloss White nor the India Ivory. The weight of the planter appears to be lighter than the other vitreous china artware items. Therefore, the planter and its mark are shown without being able to determine their value or authenticity. *Courtesy Ed Watkinson*

Underside of the elephant planter. The capital letters TEPECO are raised and under the glaze.

Bibliography

Books

Duke, Harvey. *Official Price Guide to Pottery and Porcelain.* N.Y. ,N.Y.: House of Collectibles, 1995.

Evans, Paul. *Art Pottery of the United States.* N.Y., N.Y.: Feingold & Lewis Publishing Corp., 1987

Federal Writers' Project. *New Jersey A Guide to Its Present and Past.* N.Y., N.Y.: Hastings House Publishers, 1946.

Flinchum, Russell. *Henry Dreyfuss Industrial Designer The Man In The Brown Suit.* New York: Rizzoli International Publications, Inc., 1997.

Lehner, Lois. *Lehner's Encyclopedia of U.S. Marks on Pottery, Porcelain, & Clay.* Paducah, Kentucky: Collector Books, 1988.

Lerner, Dr. M. W. "The Art Pottery of the Trenton Potteries Company." *The Antique Trader Weekly,* DuBuque, Iowa: April 13, 1983.

Levin, Anne. "Trenton's Little-Known Treasure," *The Trenton Times,* Trenton: June 6, 1995.

Paradis, Joe. *Abingdon Pottery Artware.* Atglen, Pa.: Schiffer Publishing, Ltd., 1997.

Roberts, Brenda. *The Collectors Encyclopedia of Hull Pottery.* Paducah, Kentucky: Collector Books, 1995.

Shuman, Eleanore Nolan. *The Trenton Story.* Trenton, New Jersey: MacCrellish & Quigley Company, 1958.

Tedder, Howard. "Brick Wall A Reminder of Potteries," *The Trentonian (The Evening Times)* Trenton, N.J: November 29, 1972.

Trenton Chamber of Commerce. *250th Anniversary of the Settlement of Trenton.* Trenton, N. J.: Trenton Chamber of Commerce, 1929.

The Trenton Historical Society. *A History of Trenton 1679-1929.* Princeton, N. J.: Princeton University Press, 1929.

Wolf, George A. *Industrial Trenton and Vicinity.* Wilmington, Delaware: George A. Wolf, Publisher, 1900.

Additional Sources

Cohen, Robin. "The Trenton Potteries Company, TEPECO," undated.

Crockery and Glass Journal. Various issues, dated and undated, late 1930s.

Interviews and conversations with numerous former Trenton Potteries Co. employees and their families, 1992-2000.

Trenton Potteries advertisements for TEPECO and TAC, undated.

Trenton Potteries Company (American Trent Art China), undated Catalog Publication and Price List, (1941).

Index